CASE CLOSED™

VOLUME 3

Gosho Aoyama

Case Briefing:

Subject: **Jimmy Kudo a.k.a. Conan Edogawa**
Occupation: **High School Student/Detective**
Special Skills: **Analytical thinking and deductive reasoning, Soccer**
Equipment: **Bow Tie Voice Transmitter, Super Sneakers, Homing Glasses, Stretchy Suspenders**

The subject is hot on the trail of a pair of suspicious men in black when he is attacked from behind and administered a strange substance which physically transforms him into a first grader. When the subject confides in the eccentric inventor Dr. Agasa, they decide to keep the subject's true identity a secret for the safety of everyone around him. Assuming the new identity of first-grader Conan Edogawa, the subject continues to assist the police force on their most baffling cases. The only problem is that most crime-solving professionals won't take a little kid's advice!

Table of Contents

CONFIDEN

CASE CLOSED

Volume 3 • Shonen Sunday Edition

GOSHO AOYAMA

English Adaptation
Naoko Amemiya

Translation
Joe Yamazaki

Touch-up & Lettering
Walden Wong

Cover & Graphics Design
Veronica Casson

Editor
Andy Nakatani

Original Japanese edition "MEITANTEI CONAN" published by SHOGAKUKAN Inc.

The rights of the author(s) of the work(s) in this publication to be so identified have been asserted in accordance with the Copyright, Designs and Patents Act 1988. A CIP catalogue record for this book is available from the British Library.

PARENTAL ADVISORY
CASE CLOSED is rated T+ for Older Teen and is recommended for ages 16 and up. This volume contains realistic and graphic violence.

ratings.viz.com

www.viz.com

Printed in the U.S.A.
Published by VIZ Media, LLC
P.O. Box 77010
San Francisco, CA 94107

10 9 8 7 6 5
First printing, December 2004
Fifth printing, September 2011

FILE 1: THE HATAMOTO FAMILY

WOOOO

WOW, WHAT A BEAUTIFUL VIEW! ♡

WOULDN'T YOU KNOW IT! THE ONE TIME HE FINALLY TAKES US ON A TRIP, HE SCREWS UP A MAJOR DETAIL.
WE WERE LUCKY THIS CHARTER SHIP HAPPENED TO BE AT THE ISLAND.
WE WERE *THIS CLOSE* TO BEING TRAPPED ON THAT ISLAND IN THE MIDDLE OF NOWHERE FOR THREE MORE DAYS.
SNORE ...

BUT I WONDER WHAT KIND OF PEOPLE WOULD RENT A WHOLE BIG SHIP LIKE THIS ALL TO THEMSELVES ...?

UM, IS SOMETHING WRONG ?

I'M ... I'M ALL RIGHT.
I WAS JUST THINKING ABOUT MY MOTHER AND FATHER. THEY DIED LAST YEAR IN AN ACCIDENT.

OH ...
I WAS JUST WISHING THEY COULD'VE SEEN ME IN MY WEDDING DRESS TODAY.

WEDDING DRESS ...?
WHAT'S WRONG, NATSUE ?
OH, TAKESHI ...

YOU SEE, WE GOT MARRIED TODAY !!
HEY, HEY.
M-MARRIED ...?
NATSUE HATAMOTO
SECOND DAUGHTER OF GOZO HATAMOTO'S ELDEST SON, SHOICHI. AGE 22.
TAKESHI HATAMOTO
NATSUE'S HUSBAND. EMPLOYED AT HATAMOTO BUSSAN. MARRIED INTO THE HATAMOTO FAMILY. AGE 22.

YES, AT HATAMOTO ISLAND, WHERE WE JUST WERE. WE HELD THE CEREMONY THERE THIS VERY MORNING !!
WOW! CON-GRAT-ULATIONS !!
BUT WHY WAY OUT THERE, ON THAT ISLAND ?
MOST OF THAT ISLAND BELONGS TO OUR FAMILY, THE HATAMOTO CLAN. GENERATIONS OF OUR ANCESTORS ARE ENSHRINED THERE.
FROM WAY BACK, IT'S BEEN A HATAMOTO FAMILY TRADITION TO HOLD OUR WEDDINGS ON THAT ISLAND!!
I SEE ...

WE RENTED THIS SHIP FOR OUR EXCLUSIVE USE. WHY ARE THERE OUTSIDERS ON BOARD !?
I-I'M SORRY, FATHER ...

YOU IDIOT! HOW DID THIS HAPPEN !?

THOSE PEOPLE WERE IN A FIX, SO I--
YOU HAD NO RIGHT TO DO THAT !!
HMPH
GLARE

YOU MUST BE A PRETTY BIG MAN TO MAKE DECISIONS WITHOUT MY PERMISSION!!
I-I HAD NO INTENTION OF--
GOZO HATAMOTO
DIRECTOR OF THE HATAMOTO GROUP HEAD OF THE HATAMOTO CLAN.
AGE 72.
KITARO HATAMOTO
HUSBAND OF GOZO HATAMOTO'S ELDEST DAUGHTER, MARIKO.
VICE PRESIDENT OF HATAMOTO CONSTRUCTION.
AGE 47.
MARRIED INTO THE HATAMOTO FAMILY.

WHY, YOU'VE ALWAYS BEEN ...
.....
DON'T PAY ANY ATTENTION.
SCOLD
SCOLD

GRAND-FATHER'S BEEN IN A BAD MOOD SINCE THE WEDDING RECEPTION.
EVER SINCE HE ATE MY FOOD.

UNCLE JOJI ...

JOJIJ HATAMOTO
GOZO HATAMOTO'S SECOND SON . FRENCH CHEF. SINGLE. AGE 41.

I KNEW DAD HATED WESTERN FOOD BUT ...

WHAT IS THIS!? IT'S *PIG SLOP*!!

... I DIDN'T THINK HE'D GET *THAT* MAD.

PERHAPS I'M NOT SKILLED ENOUGH YET.

NO, NOT AT ALL !!

EVERY-THING WAS REALLY DELICIOUS !!

ICHIRO HATAMOTO
ONLY SON OF KITARO HATAMOTO.
ART STUDENT.
AGE 21.
SKCH
SKCH

TWITCH
LIKE FATHER, LIKE SON !!

HOW COULD YOU LET HIM WASTE TIME AS A WANNABE ARTIST?
YOU'RE HIS FATHER ... TELL HIM STRAIGHT !!
IT'S TIME TO ABANDON HIS UNATTAIN-ABLE DREAMS !!

HEY, TAKESHI ...
S-SIR ?

I'D LIKE A WORD WITH YOU... COME TO MY ROOM LATER.
Y-YES, SIR !!
?

.....
JUST BEAR IT FOR NOW, DEAR ...
FATHER IS OLD. HE WON'T BE AROUND FOR MUCH LONGER.

AND *THEN*, NOW THAT ELDER BROTHER SHOICHI IS DEAD, THE MAJORITY OF THE HATAMOTO GROUP'S WEALTH AND THE FAMILY FORTUNE WILL BE...
... YOURS.
MARIKO HATAMOTO
GOZO HATAMOTO'S ELDEST DAUGHTER. KITARO'S WIFE.
AGE 43

IT WON'T BE THAT EASY ...

... AUNT MARIKO.
A- AKIE ...

TATSUO HEARD FROM SUZUKI THE BUTLER LAST NIGHT.
HE HEARD WHAT GRAND-FATHER PLANS TO DO WITH THE COMPANY AND THE FORTUNE.
HA! DIDN'T TAKE MUCH OF A THREAT TO GET THAT SENILE BUTLER TO SPILL HIS GUTS.
CHMP
CHMP
AKIE HATAMOTO
DAUGHTER OF GOZO HATA-MOTO'S ELDEST SON, SHOICHI. NATSUE'S OLDER SISTER.
AGE 26.
TATSUO HATAMOTO
HUSBAND OF AKIE. MUSICIAN. MARRIED INTO THE HATAMOTO FAMILY.
AGE 26.

PSST
PSST

SO? WHAT'S FATHER GOT UP HIS SLEEVE?
HMPH ... DON'T BE SHOCKED NOW.
TOINK

!?

N-NO ...! THAT CAN'T BE.
GRAND-FATHER'S PLANNING ON ANNOUNCING IT WHEN WE ARRIVE IN TOKYO.

THIS IS INSANE!
I MEAN, WE'RE STUCK RUNNIN' AROUND FROM DEBT COLLECTORS.
PTUI

BUT THERE'S 24 HOURS LEFT UNTIL THIS SHIP ARRIVES IN TOKYO.
THAT'S HOW LONG WE HAVE ...

... TO DO SOME-THING ABOUT THIS.

WOOO

NOK NOK
OH, TAKESHI ...?
COME IN.

EXCUSE ME, SIR!
CLICK
YOUR SPEECH TODAY AT THE WEDDING RECEPTION WAS EXCELLENT!!

NO WONDER NATSUE CHOSE YOU.
WELL, ER ...

HO HOH... THAT HABIT OF SCRATCHING YOUR CHEEK WHEN YOU'RE EMBARRASSED.
YOU HAVE THE EXACT SAME HABIT ...

... AS YOUR FATHER --
ISAO ZAIKI!!!

NOW TELL ME! WHAT IS YOUR OBJECTIVE ?

.....
YOU CAN TAMPER WITH YOUR FAMILY REGISTRY ...
... BUT YOU CAN'T FOOL ME !!

I'VE KNOWN FOR A WHILE NOW.
YOU JOINED THE COMPANY AND GOT CLOSE TO NATSUE TO AVENGE YOUR FATHER.

IS IT MONEY !?
OR ...
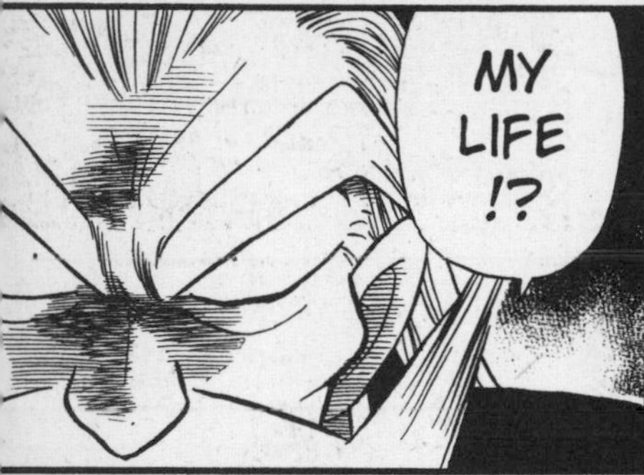
MY LIFE !?
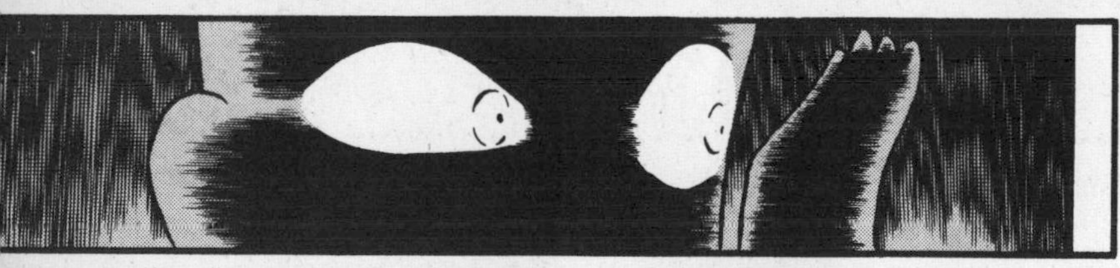

ANSWER ME !!

WOOOO

Gozo Hatamoto
Eldest Son
Shoichi
Miyuki
Eldest Daughter
Mariko
Kitaro
2nd Son
Joji
Eldest Daughter
Akie
Tatsuo
2nd Daughter
Natsue
Takeshi
Ichiro

THESE ARE THE MEMBERS OF THE MAIN HOUSE OF THE HATAMOTO CLAN.

WOW, SO THESE PEOPLE ALL ATTENDED YOUR WEDDING?
YES, NINE PEOPLE. EVERYONE BESIDES MY DECEASED FATHER SHOICHI AND MOTHER MIYUKI.

IN A LITTLE WHILE, ALL OF THEM WILL COME DOWN FOR DINNER.
I'LL INTRO-DUCE YOU TO THEM THEN.
WHAT'S TAKING TAKESHI SO LONG ...?
YES... HE'S BEEN IN GRAND-FATHER'S ROOM THIS WHOLE TIME.
I WONDER WHAT'S GOING ON.

OH, THEY'RE PROBABLY DISCUSSING SOMETHING SHADY.

A-AKIE !!

HMPH...
YOU'RE LATE, ICHIRO. YOU WASHED YOUR HANDS, I HOPE?
CLUNK
SCOOT
MM?
DAD'S NOT HERE YET?
NO... BUT I BELIEVE HE'LL BE HERE SHORTLY.
KENJI SUZUKI
HATAMOTO FAMILY BUTLER.
AGE 64.
HEY, YOU'RE LATE.
SORRY...
SKOOT

SO, RACHEL...

DO YOU HAVE A BOYFRIEND?
HUH...?

NAH, FAR FROM IT... RACHEL'S STILL A KID.
EXCUSE ME!

I DO TOO HAVE SOMEBODY I LIKE!!
RIGHT, CONAN!?
ER, YEAH...

MY! WHAT'S HE LIKE ?
WELL... HE'S SMART, GOOD AT SOCCER..

YOU CAN COUNT ON HIM IN A PINCH, AND HE'S VERY CUTE...
EH HEH HEH ...
WHAT ARE *YOU* BLUSHING FOR ?

AND HE'S AS GOOD A PRIVATE DETECTIVE AS DAD !!
HM ?
SO YOUR FATHER IS A ...

OH, DIDN'T I TELL YOU ?
MY FATHER'S A PRIVATE DETEC-TIVE.
GRIN

!?
!?
!?

WH-
WHAT'S
THE
MATTER
...?

SHHH!
GRAND-
FATHER
DESPISES
DETEC-
TIVES.
HUH
?
HE SAYS
PEOPLE WHO
SNEAK AROUND
AND DIG UP THE
PRIVATE AFFAIRS
OF OTHERS ARE
NO GOOD.

THAT'S WHY
NOBODY IN THE
HATAMOTO FAMILY
IS ALLOWED TO
WATCH DETECTIVE
SHOWS OR READ
MYSTERY
NOVELS.
HMM
...
PLEASE
DON'T
MENTION
THIS TO
GRAND-
FATHER
...

SIR,
DINNER
IS
READY
...
KNOCK
KNOCK
SIR
?

HMM
?

A
FLOWER
...?

SORRY ...
I WAS IN THE ROOM DOING SOME THINKING.
SKOOT
ARE YOU OKAY? YOU LOOK KIND OF PALE.

TAKESHI !
SHUFF
YOU'RE QUITE LATE ...

HEY. YOUR FLOWER ...
THAT'S STRANGE ...
WHERE DID IT GO ?

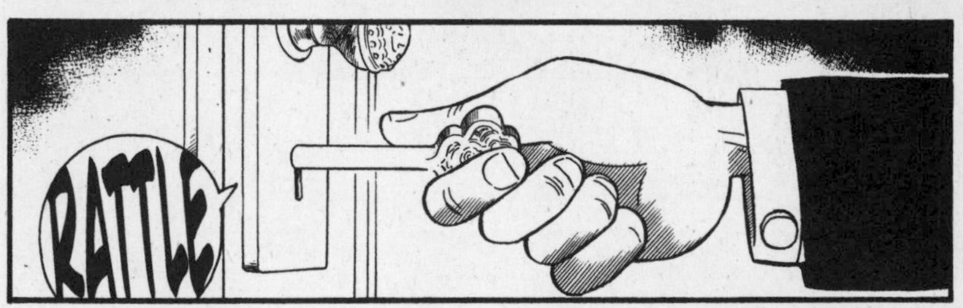
RATTLE

SIR ...
KCHAK
EVERY-BODY IS WAITING FOR--

!?

AAAIII

WHAT WAS THAT !?
WASN'T THAT SUZUKI'S VOICE?
FROM DAD'S ROOM !?

DA DA DA DA

WHAT'S WRONG, SUZUKI !?
AH ...
AIII ...

FILE 2: THE SECRET OF THE LOCKED ROOM

DAMN IT.
HE'S DEAD.
NO ...
NO !!
GRAND-FATHER !!
OH ...

STOP RIGHT THERE !!

LISTEN! NOBODY STEPS FOOT IN THIS ROOM!

NOT UNTIL I SAY SO !!

RIGOR MORTIS HAS NOT SET IN HIS JAWS YET.
BUT THE PUPILLARY SPHINCTER MUSCLES ARE STARTING TO TIGHTEN UP.
AND CONSIDERING THE DROP IN HIS BODY TEMPERATURE ...

I CONCLUDE THAT MR. GOZO DIED ABOUT ...
... 40 TO 50 MINUTES AGO.

HMM, PRETTY KNOWLEDGE-ABLE FOR A DETECTIVE.
MY DAD USED TO WORK AS A HOMICIDE DETEC-TIVE.

MR. SUZUKI ... IT WAS YOU, HIS BUTLER, WHO DISCOVERED THE BODY, CORRECT ?
Y-YES ...
WHERE WERE YOU 40 TO 50 MINUTES AGO ?
IN OTHER WORDS, AT APPROXIMATELY 8 O'CLOCK.
AROUND 8 O'CLOCK I WAS IN THE DINING HALL PREPARING FOR DINNER.

YOU BETTER NOT BE LYING!
I-IT'S TRUE !!
YOU CAN ASK THE OTHER PEOPLE ON STAFF.

HE'S NOT LYING !
MR. SUZUKI WAS BUSY DOING STUFF AROUND OUR TABLE AT THAT TIME.
RIGHT, NATSUE ?
UH, YES ...

WHEN YOU DISCOVERED THE BODY, YOU'RE SURE THE DOOR WAS LOCKED ?
YES, IT WAS.
TELL ME. HOW IS THIS DOOR LOCKED?
IT CAN BE LOCKED BY HAND FROM INSIDE. BUT FROM THE OUTSIDE YOU'D NEED THIS KEY.
IS THERE ANOTHER COPY OF THE KEY FOR THIS ROOM ?
NO, THIS IS THE ONLY ONE.
MR. GOZO GAVE IT TO ME FOR SAFE-KEEPING WHEN WE BOARDED THE SHIP.

THE WINDOWS OF THIS ROOM DON'T OPEN ...
... AND THE ONLY DOOR TO THE ROOM WAS LOCKED.
IT WOULD'VE BEEN IMPOSSIBLE TO BREAK IN FROM THE OUTSIDE.

IN OTHER WORDS, THIS ROOM WAS COMPLETELY SEALED !!
S-SEALED !?
BUT IF NOBODY COULD'VE GOTTEN IN ...
... THAT MEANS ...

IT WAS SUICIDE !?

DO YOU KNOW OF ANY REASONS WHY MR. GOZO MAY HAVE TAKEN HIS OWN LIFE ?
TH-THAT CAN'T BE. GRAND-FATHER WOULDN'T KILL HIMSELF!
HMPH ... YOU NEVER KNOW ...
I HEAR THE OLD MAN'S DONE SOME PRETTY BAD THINGS IN THE PAST.

MAYBE HE TRIED TO REPENT FOR THE MULTITUDE OF HIS SINS BY STABBING HIMSELF AT HIS GRAND-DAUGHTER'S WEDDING !!
T-TATSUO.
I CAN'T SEE DAD DOING THAT...
OH, REALLY ?

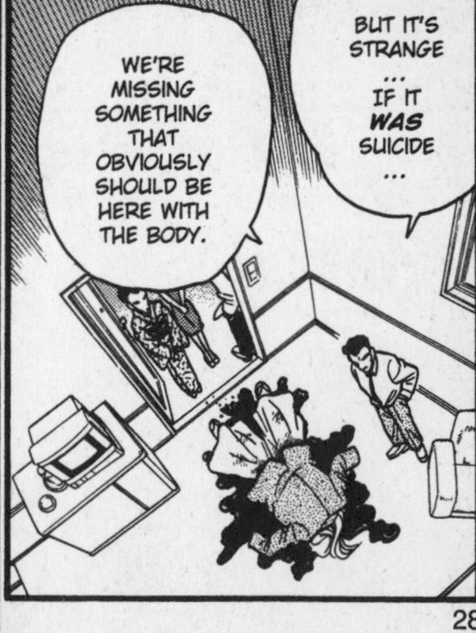
BUT IT'S STRANGE ... IF IT WAS SUICIDE ...
WE'RE MISSING SOMETHING THAT OBVIOUSLY SHOULD BE HERE WITH THE BODY.

WHAT ?

THE WEAPON.

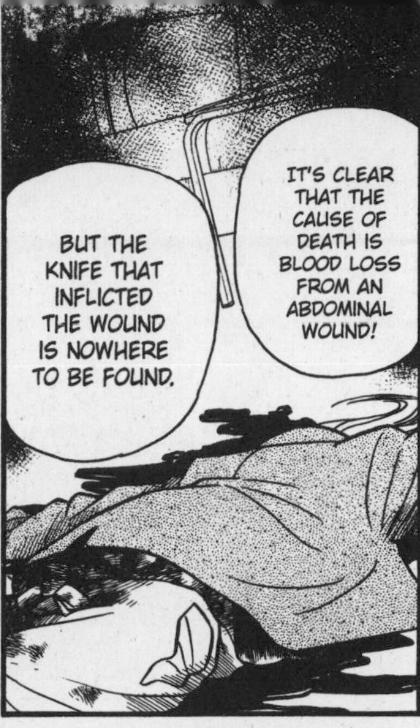
IT'S CLEAR THAT THE CAUSE OF DEATH IS BLOOD LOSS FROM AN ABDOMINAL WOUND!
BUT THE KNIFE THAT INFLICTED THE WOUND IS NOWHERE TO BE FOUND.

WHERE COULD IT BE?
PROBABLY A SHARP PIECE OF ICE OR SOMETHING, HUH?

YOU KNOW, LIKE IN THE MYSTERY NOVELS.
THE WEAPON THAT VANISHES WITH TIME...

WHY WOULD SOMEONE COMMITTING SUICIDE DO SOMETHING LIKE THAT?
I BET GRANDFATHER DID IT TO SPITE US!!

HE WANTED TO THROW SUSPICION ON EVERY MEMBER OF THE HATAMOTO CLAN, JUST TO CAUSE US GRIEF.
GRANDFATHER HATED EVERYBODY IN THE FAMILY!

EVERYBODY BESIDES ***NATSUE***, THAT IS.
A-AKIE...

HMM, I ***COULD*** SEE DAD DOING THAT.
U-UNCLE JOJI, YOU TOO?
IT ***WAS*** SUICIDE, THEN! IT'S SETTLED!!

NO, THIS WAS MURDER...

GASP!
CONAN!?
AND A VERY SIMPLE ONE AT THAT.
WHAT!?
Y-YOU AGAIN!
HERE, TAKE A LOOK.
RIGHT IN THE DOORWAY...
LOOK AT THIS BLOOD...

SO IT'S NATURAL TO CONCLUDE HE WAS STABBED WHEN THE DOOR WAS OPEN.
I-I SEE ...

MM ?
IF THE DOOR WAS CLOSED WHEN THE GRANDFATHER KILLED HIMSELF ...
... THERE WOULDN'T BE ANY BLOOD HERE, RIGHT?

MR. GOZO WAS STABBED BY SOMEBODY THE MOMENT HE WAS ABOUT TO LEAVE THE ROOM!!
THEN WHO LOCKED THE DOOR ?

MM ?
.....

HUH ?
GLARE

THAT'S RIGHT ... WHO LOCKED THE DOOR ?
YOU'RE SUPPOSED TO TELL US!
WHACK

!?
OF COURSE !!

MR. GOZO LOCKED THE DOOR HIMSELF!!
WHAT !?

HE MUST HAVE BEEN STABBED BY SOMEBODY OUTSIDE THE ROOM.
SHHHK
TO ESCAPE FROM THE ASSAILANT, HE FLED INTO THE ROOM.
HE WAS ABLE TO LOCK THE DOOR ...
AND THEN HE RAN OUT OF STRENGTH AND DIED !!
SLUMP

THE LOCKED ROOM, THE LACK OF A MURDER WEAPON, AND THE BLOOD IN THE GROOVE OF THE DOOR ...
EVERY-THING FITS THIS EXPLANA-TION !!!
HMM ...
INDEED ...

WOW, YOU REALLY ARE A GREAT DETECTIVE !!
HA HA HA !!

HA ...

WAIT A SEC ...
THEN THAT MEANS EVERY-BODY HAD AN OPPORTUNITY TO DO IT.

THE MURDER WAS COMMITTED AROUND 8:00 PM.
THAT'S RIGHT AROUND THE TIME EVERY-BODY STARTED TO GATHER FOR DINNER.

THE FOUR OF US, NATSUE, RACHEL, CONAN, AND I, WERE SEATED AT OUR TABLE BY AROUND 7:30. IT WOULD HAVE BEEN IMPOSSIBLE FOR ANY OF US TO HAVE COMMITTED THE CRIME.

THE SAME CAN BE SAID OF MR. SUZUKI, WHO WAS NEAR OUR TABLE AT THAT TIME.

IN OTHER WORDS, THE MUR-DERER ...
... WAS NOT AT THE DINING HALL AT THAT TIME.

ONE OF THE SEVEN OF YOU IS THE MURDERER !!

MR. SUZUKI, DID YOU NOTICE ANYTHING WHEN YOU ENTERED THE ROOM ?
NO, NOTHING IN PARTICULAR.
I SHOUTED RIGHT AWAY, AND EVERYBODY CAME RUNNING.

OH ...!

A- ACTUALLY, IN FRONT OF THE DOOR ...
SHFF

... I FOUND THIS FLOWER.

!?

THAT F-FLOWER ?
IT'S THE ONE I PUT ON TAKESHI'S COAT!

WHOOSH

COME TO THINK OF IT, BUDDY... YOU WERE PRETTY LATE COMING TO THE DINING HALL.
C-C'MON, AKIE...
I-I WAS IN THE ROOM DOING SOME THINKING.

YOU DID LOOK LIKE YOU'D JUST SEEN A GHOST...
I-ICHIRO...

GIVE IT UP, TAKESHI.
WHAT?

WHEN I WAS OUTSIDE THE ROOM, I ACCIDENTALLY OVERHEARD YOU!!

YOU AND FATHER WERE ARGUING!!

!?

A-ARGUING?
I THOUGHT MY LEGS WOULD GIVE OUT.

I HEARD THIS MAN'S REAL IDENTITY!

HE'S ACTUALLY ISAO ZAIKI'S SON !!

TAKESHI !?

BUT TO THINK THAT CHILD WAS TAKESHI ...
.....
I-IS THAT TRUE, TAKESHI !?

IT'S ...
IT'S TRUE.

I AM ISAO ZAIKI'S SON.
I'M TAKEHIKO ZAIKI !!!

B-BUT I ...
I SEE. YOU COZIED UP TO NATSUE TO SNEAK YOUR WAY INTO THE HATAMOTO FAMILY SO YOU COULD AVENGE YOUR FATHER.
YOU WERE SECRETLY WAITING FOR YOUR CHANCE TO KILL MR. GOZO.

AND TONIGHT ...

YOU CARRIED IT OUT !!
N-NO !!
I DIDN'T KILL HIM !!
DASH
WAAAA!!
NATSUE, I DIDN'T DO IT !
GRAB
NATSUE !!

HEH! PRETTY STUPID TO DROP YOUR FLOWER AT THE SCENE OF THE CRIME!!
I DON'T KNOW WHEN I LOST THAT FLOWER...
HO HO HOH... I KNOW WHEN! WHEN YOU KILLED GRAND-FATHER!
I THOUGHT YOU WERE A GUY WITH SOME METTLE...
BUT I GUESS I SIZED YOU UP WRONG.
U-UNCLE JOJI.
NO!! IT WASN'T ME!!
STAY AWAY FROM US, YOU MURDERER!!!
LISTEN TO ME!!
!?
THERE'S BEEN BLOOD WIPED AWAY FROM THE OUTSIDE OF THE ROOM.
HEY, IS THIS REALLY WHERE YOU FOUND THAT FLOWER?
YES, THAT'S RIGHT MY BOY.

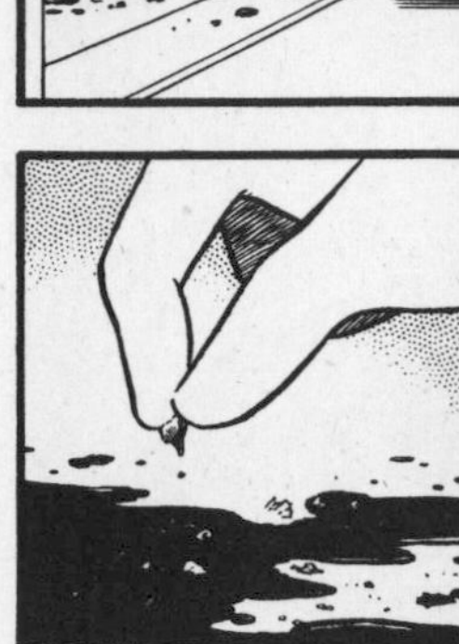

!?
PLEASE BELIEVE ME !!
I DIDN'T DO IT !!

IT WASN'T ME!
I DIDN'T KILL HIM!!

WHAT !?
WHAT'S THIS !?

FILE 3:
WHO GETS THE FORTUNE?

DASH

N-NO, NATSUE!

IT WASN'T ME!!

WAAHH!!

I DIDN'T KILL YOUR GRANDFATHER!

IT WASN'T ME!!!

A BREAD CRUMB !?

NAMELY, MASTER JOJI!!
...

EVERY-BODY ATE SOME ?
YES, EVERY-BODY EXCEPT FOR MASTER GOZO.

HE HATED WESTERN FOOD.
ESPECIALLY BREAD. SAID THE MERE SIGHT OF IT MADE HIM NAUSEOUS.
HMM ...

IF MR. JOJI IS A CHEF, HE MUST HAVE HIS OWN SET OF KNIVES, RIGHT?
HE DOES. HE ALWAYS KEEPS HIS BELOVED SET BY HIS SIDE.

HMM ...
...

NOW, NOW... A YOUNG BOY SHOULDN'T STICK HIS NOSE INTO THINGS!!
UH, OKAY.

SHFFF
CRSHHH

WHY DON'T YOU COOL YOUR HEAD IN THIS STORAGE ROOM!!
BOOT

CLANK

OPEN THE DOOR! IT WASN'T ME!!
BAM
BAM
BAM
SHUT UP, MUR-DERER !!
WHEN WE GET TO TOKYO TOMORROW, WE'RE HANDING YOU OVER TO THE COPS!!

OPEN THE DOOR !!
BAM
BAM
YOU'VE GOT ENOUGH MOTIVE AND EVIDENCE AGAINST HIM, RIGHT, MR. DETECTIVE?
YEAH ...

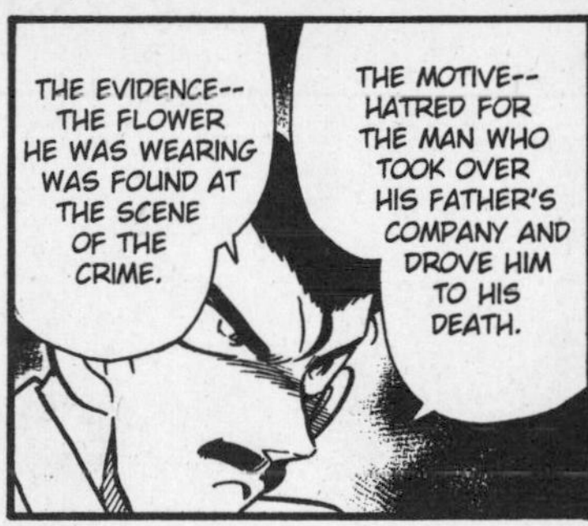
THE MOTIVE-- HATRED FOR THE MAN WHO TOOK OVER HIS FATHER'S COMPANY AND DROVE HIM TO HIS DEATH.
THE EVIDENCE-- THE FLOWER HE WAS WEARING WAS FOUND AT THE SCENE OF THE CRIME.

IF WE COULD ONLY FIND HIS PRINTS ON THE MURDER WEAPON OUR EVIDENCE WOULD BE INDISPUTABLE.

AH, WELL. IT'S PROBABLY AT THE BOTTOM OF THE OCEAN BY NOW.

HO HO HOH... AREN'T YOU LUCKY, AUNT MARIKO?

NOW THAT TAKESHI HAS KILLED GRAND-FATHER...
THE OLD MAN WON'T BE MAKING THAT STUPID ANNOUNCEMENT ABOUT HIS FORTUNE!!
HEH HEH HEH .... YOU'RE RIGHT.

THE HATAMOTO GROUP NOW BELONGS TO YOU, AS THE ELDEST DAUGHTER'S HUSBAND!

AND YOU, ICHIRO.... YOU CAN PAINT AS MUCH AS YOU WANT NOW WITHOUT BEING AFRAID OF YOUR GRANDFATHER!

AND EVENTUALLY, THE HATAMOTO GROUP WILL BE YOURS.
I-I'M NOT INTERESTED IN THAT ...

HANG ON, HERE. YOU'RE NOT PLANNING TO HOARD ALL THE OLD MAN'S FORTUNE FOR YOURSELF, ARE YOU?
DON'T YOU WORRY! YOU GRANDKIDS WILL ALSO--

THAT'S ENOUGH, MARIKO! QUIT TALKING ABOUT MONEY ON THE NIGHT OF DAD'S DEATH.

HMPH! STOP ACTING LIKE YOU'RE MR. VIRTUOUS. YOU'RE THE ONE WHO LEFT THE HATAMOTO FAMILY WITHOUT APPROVAL TO BECOME A CHEF!!

I KNOW WHAT HAPPENED.

YOU WENT TO FATHER AND ASKED TO BORROW MONEY TO OPEN YOUR RESTAURANT.
AND FATHER HARSHLY TURNED YOU DOWN !!
!?

TO NATSUE !?

YES... AND THE HATAMOTO GROUP WILL BE ENTRUSTED TO THE PERSON OF HER CHOOSING.
TH-THAT'S ABSURD ...
DAMN IT, WHAT NOW !?
KLONK
NOW I DON'T EVEN KNOW WHY I MARRIED AKIE IN THE FIRST PLACE!!
WH-WHAT DOES THAT MEAN ?

YOU DIDN'T MARRY ME TO GET AT GRANDFATHER'S MONEY, DID YOU?
I SURE DID !!
WHY ELSE WOULD I GET HITCHED TO AN EXPENSIVE HUSSY LIKE YOU !!
LOOK WHO'S TALKING, YOU NO-TALENT POSER OF A MUSICIAN! IT WOULDN'T KILL YOU TO WORK A LITTLE!!
SHUT UP !!
C'MON, YOU TWO ...

WE CAPTURED THE MURDERER ALREADY.
WHY DON'T ALL OF YOU GET SOME SLEEP NOW?

HEH ...
LOOKS LIKE DAD PULLED A FAST ONE ON US ...

HA HA HA HA HA ...

THE HELL WITH THIS!

I'VE GOTTEN THIS FAR AND I'M NOT LETTING THE ESTATE FALL THROUGH MY FINGERTIPS !!!

CRSHHH FSHHH

NATSUE ...

WHAT'RE YOU DOING OUT HERE ?
NOTHING ...
JUST THINKING ABOUT THINGS.

WOOOH
ABOUT TAKESHI ...?

...

I ...
I ...

I TRUSTED HIM.
I TRUSTED TAKESHI ... BUT ...

THEY'RE SAYING HE MARRIED ME TO KILL GRAND-FATHER!

I DON'T KNOW WHO TO TRUST.
I JUST CAN'T BELIEVE ANYBODY!!!

SNIFF ... SNIFF ...

SOB ...

I BELIEVE HIM!

IT'S JUST A FEELING.
WHAT ...?
BUT I DON'T THINK TAKESHI IS A BAD PERSON.

YOU CHOSE HIM, RIGHT, NATSUE?
SO HOW COULD HE BE A BAD PERSON!?

RACHEL ...

!?

HEY, DID YOU HEAR A STRANGE SOUND JUST NOW?
HUH?

DID YOU HEAR SOME-THING, NATSUE?
NO, NOTHING ...
I'M SURE I HEARD SOME-THING!!

THE SPLASH OF SOMETHING FALLING INTO THE WATER, AND A DULL, CREEPY THUD.
IT CAME FROM THE DECK BELOW!!

I'M GONNA TAKE A LOOK !!!

DASH

C- CONAN !

WAIT UP !

DA DA DA

CONAN !!

WAIT, YOU TWO ...

WHAT ARE YOU --?

TMP TMP ...

!?

KYAAAAAA
HUH ...?

DASH

H-HEY, CONAN!

DA DA DA DA

IT'S OPEN!!

FWAM

!?
NEGISHI KIKAI
HE'S ...
HE'S GONE !!!

FILE 4: FAMILY MASSACRE

H-
HONEY
...

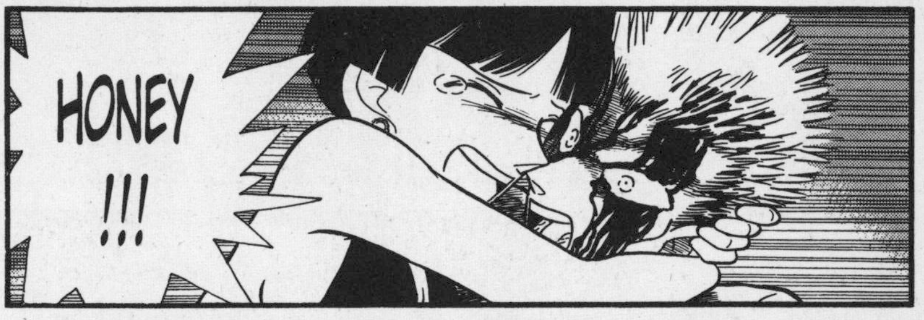
HONEY
!!!

AAAAAH
...

OH, MR. DETECTIVE ...
SO ...?

WAS TAKESHI THERE ?
W-WELL ...

WHAT
!?
HE WASN'T IN THE STORAGE ROOM
!?

I'M SURE THERE WAS NO WAY OUT WITH THE DOOR LOCKED FROM THE OUTSIDE, BUT...
HE WAS NOWHERE TO BE FOUND.

TH-THEN THAT MEANS ...
THE ONE WHO KILLED BOTH FATHER AND TATSUO WAS...

TAKESHI
!?

RACHEL, CONAN, AND NATSUE DISCOVERED THE BODY, RIGHT?
YES
!
THE THREE OF US WERE TALKING ON THE UPPER DECK.
THEN CONAN SAID HE HEARD SOMETHING STRANGE AND RAN OFF.
WE CAME DOWN TO THIS DECK ...

AND FOUND TATSUO DEAD.

WHAT KIND OF STRANGE SOUND DID YOU HEAR?
A SPLASH OF SOMETHING FALLING INTO THE WATER AND THEN A DULL THUD !

HMM ...

THE CAUSE OF DEATH IS PROBABLY BRAIN CONTUSIONS FROM AN IMPACT TO THE HEAD.
JUDGING FROM THE WOUND, HE MUST HAVE BEEN HIT BY SOMETHING LIKE A LEAD PIPE.

THAT DULL THUD CONAN HEARD WAS PROBABLY THE SOUND OF THE MURDERER STRIKING TATSUO.
THE SPLASH COULD HAVE BEEN THE WEAPON DROPPING INTO THE OCEAN, OR ...

MAYBE THE MURDERER JUMPED, REALIZING HE HAD NO PLACE TO RUN.
OH ...

TAKESHI ...

I WANT EVERYONE TO TAKE REFUGE IN THE DINING HALL !!
IN ANY EVENT, THERE'S A GREAT CHANCE THE MURDERER IS STILL LURKING ON BOARD !!
HUH? US TOO?

THERE'S NO REASON WHY TAKESHI WOULD BE AFTER OUR LIVES.
HAVE YOU FOR-GOTTEN ?

THE MOTIVE FOR HIS CRIME WAS HIS HATRED FOR THE HEAD OF THE HATAMOTO FAMILY. GOZO HATAMOTO IS THE MAN WHO TOOK OVER HIS FATHER'S COMPANY, DRIVING HIM TO HIS DEATH TEN YEARS AGO.
IT COULD BE THAT ...

HE'S PLANNING A MASSACRE !
A MASSACRE OF THE ENTIRE HATAMOTO FAMILY!!

NO ...
NO ...

HURRY, EVERY-ONE !
...
WHAT'S THE MATTER ? LET'S GO, CONAN !

HMM ... OKAY.

IT HASN'T BEEN DETERMINED YET THAT TAKESHI IS THE MURDERER.

WHAT !?
ZOOM

C-CONAN ?
REMEMBER? WHEN WE GOT TO THE STORAGE ROOM WHERE TAKESHI WAS CONFINED, IT WAS UNLOCKED, RIGHT?
Y-YEAH.

SOMEONE MUST HAVE OPENED THAT LOCK FROM THE OUTSIDE. HE COULDN'T HAVE UNLOCKED IT FROM INSIDE!
YOU HAVE A POINT. THERE WAS NO SIGN OF IT BEING FORCED, EITHER.

BUT IF SOMEBODY OPENED IT ...
IT MUST MEAN ...

THERE'S AN ACCOMPLICE HERE...!

THE ENGINE ROOM...
VROM
VROM
VROM

HUF
HUF
HUF

HUF
HUF
HUF

WELL, LET'S SEE NOW...

AT THE TIME THAT CONAN HEARD THE DULL SOUND, IN OTHER WORDS, AT THE TIME OF THE CRIME...

YOU THREE WERE EACH ALONE, RESTING IN YOUR ROOMS.

YOU TWO MARRIED FOLKS WERE THE ONLY ONES SHARING A ROOM.

Y-YES, BUT JUST AROUND THEN I HAD GONE TO THE MEN'S ROOM...

SO IT'S THE SAME AS WITH THE FIRST MURDER.

NATSUE WAS WITH CONAN AND RACHEL, BUT EVERYONE ELSE...

... HAS NO ALIBI !!

Y-YOU GOTTA BE JOKING!! IT WAS MY HUSBAND THAT WAS JUST KILLED !!
HOW DARE YOU INCLUDE *ME* AS A SUSPECT !!

HMPH. AREN'T YOU THE ONE WHO'S MOST RELIEVED BY TATSUO'S DEATH, AKIE?
WHAT ?

I KNOW ALL ABOUT IT !!
I KNOW YOU HAVE ANOTHER GUY !!
!?

!?

THAT LADY KNOWS EVERY-THING ...
AND WEREN'T YOU JUST FIGHTING WITH TATSUO TONIGHT ?
THAT'S JUST 'CUZ OF THE FORTUNE ISSUE ...

PLEASE !!
FLIP
FLIP

YOU HAD PLENTY OF MOTIVE TO KILL GRAND-FATHER, TOO !!
BESIDES, YOU'RE THE ONE, AUNT MARIKO, WHO WAS MOST OBSESSED ABOUT THE FORTUNE!

STOP IT, YOU TWO ...

WOW, DID YOU DRAW THAT? IT'S NATSUE, RIGHT ?
FLINCH
!?

HUH ?
FWIP

HMPH! AUNT MARIKO'S SON ICHIRO IS NO EXCEPTION EITHER !!
THINK ABOUT IT!

YOU WERE PRACTICALLY SOBBING WHEN THE OLD MAN TORE UP THAT PRIZE-WINNING PAINTING OF YOURS !!!
!?

FATHER WAS WRONG IN REFUSING TO ACKNOW-LEDGE THIS BOY'S TALENT !!
HMPH! AND NOT ONLY THAT, BUT ...
YOU DIDN'T LIKE IT WHEN TATSUO PICKED ON YOU, RIGHT ?
HE CALLED YOU A GLOOMY GEEK AND--
N- NO !
IT WASN'T ME !!
I DIDN'T KILL HIM !!

HEH HEH HEH. AND THE PERSON WHO MOST LONGED TO BE FREE FROM GRANDFATHER WAS YOU.
ISN'T THAT RIGHT, *UNCLE KITARO* ?
WH- WHAT ARE YOU SAYING ?
THAT'S ENOUGH !!

THIS SHIP WILL ARRIVE IN TOKYO IN HALF A DAY!!
WHEN IT DOES, IF TAKESHI IS ALIVE, HE WON'T BE ABLE TO RUN OR HIDE, AND THE FACTS OF THIS CASE WILL BE REVEALED!!
UNTIL THEN, I WANT YOU PEOPLE TO REMAIN CALM! I DON'T WANT ANYTHING ELSE TO HAPPEN!!
......
SKOOT
WH-WHERE ARE YOU GOING, ICHIRO?
THE RESTROOM.
YOU OKAY BY YOURSELF?

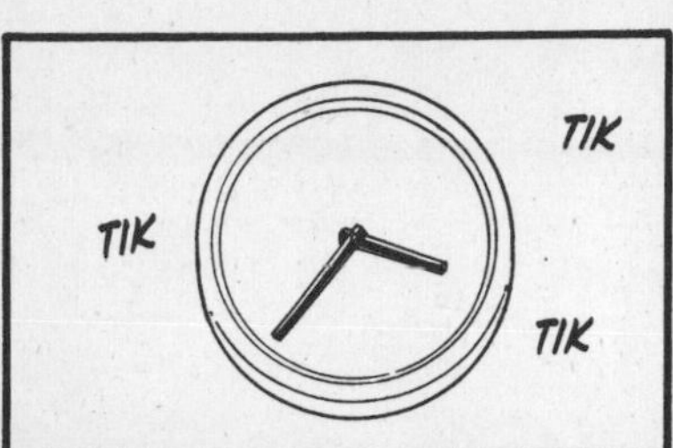

HEY MR. DETECTIVE. WHAT DO YOU THINK OF THIS POSSIBILITY?

THE WAY THINGS WERE, ALL OF THE FORTUNE WOULD GO TO NATSUE AS WRITTEN IN THE WILL.
TATSUO, HUNG UP ON THE FORTUNE, WENT TO THE STORAGE ROOM, OPENED THE LOCK, AND OFFERED TAKESHI A DEAL, "I'LL PROVIDE FALSE TESTIMONY TO PROVE YOUR INNOCENCE, IF YOU GIVE ME THE FORTUNE."
AS NATSUE'S HUSBAND, IF HE IS FOUND INNOCENT THE FORTUNE WOULD BE AS MUCH HIS AS NATSUE'S.

TAKESHI, PRETENDING TO ACCEPT THE OFFER, PROCEEDED TO LURE TATSUO OUT TO THE DECK AND ...
WHACK!
IT DOESN'T SEEM TOO MUCH OF A STRETCH TO IMAGINE IT THIS WAY, DON'T YOU THINK?
I- INDEED ...
IT'S POSSIBLE, CON-SIDERING THAT TATSUO'S PERSONAL-ALITY.

SO YOU'RE SAYING ...
IT WAS TAKESHI ...?
TAKESHI ...

ER ... UM ...
ICHIRO HASN'T RETURNED FROM THE RESTROOM YET.

WHAT !?
IT'S BEEN AROUND TWENTY MINUTES NOW.
WHAT IF ...

TAKESHI GOT TO HIM !?
CALM DOWN! HE COULD JUST BE TAKING A LONG TIME.

CLICK
I'LL GO TAKE A LOOK.

FSH HH

FSHHH

BINK

BINK
HUH ?

I-IT'S A BLACK-OUT !!
KYAAAA!
P-PLEASE EVERYBODY, STAY CALM! STAY RIGHT WHERE YOU ARE!!
BUT, ICHIRO IS STILL IN THE RESTROOM.

I- ICHIRO !!
WHOA! MA'AM, NO! DON'T LEAVE THE ROOM!!
DASH...

WAIT!!
TMP TMP TMP
KYAA! KYAA!

DARN IT! RACHEL, CONAN, YOU GUYS HERE?
YEAH !
I'M RIGHT HERE !

I'M GOING TO THE ELEC-TRICAL ROOM !
YOU GUYS HEAD TO THE RESTROOM TO FIND ICHIRO !!
OKAY, WE'RE ON IT !!
TA TA TA...
THE RESTROOM IS THIS WAY, RIGHT ?
YEAH !
TA TA TA TA...

AAAARGH
!?

WASN'T THAT ICHIRO'S VOICE!?
DARN !!
DASH...
WH-★ACK

GASP !

FLIK

OW ...

ICHIRO !?

ICHIRO !!!

UNGH ...

FILE 5: WHO RIGGED THE DARKNESS?

ARE YOU ALL RIGHT, ICHIRO!?
YOU OKAY!?
UNGH...

DID YOU GET AN IMPRESSION OF THE ASSAILANT'S FACE OR HEIGHT?
IT WAS PITCH BLACK. I COULDN'T SEE A THING.

YOU DIDN'T SEE A FLASH OF LIGHT OR ANYTHING?
N-NO, NOTHING LIKE THAT.
!?

OH ...
WHAT'S THIS !?

GEORGE'S KNIFE !?
George.H

TH- THIS IS INDEED MINE ...
GEORGE, IT WASN'T *YOU* WHO ATTACKED ICHIRO ... *WAS IT !?*

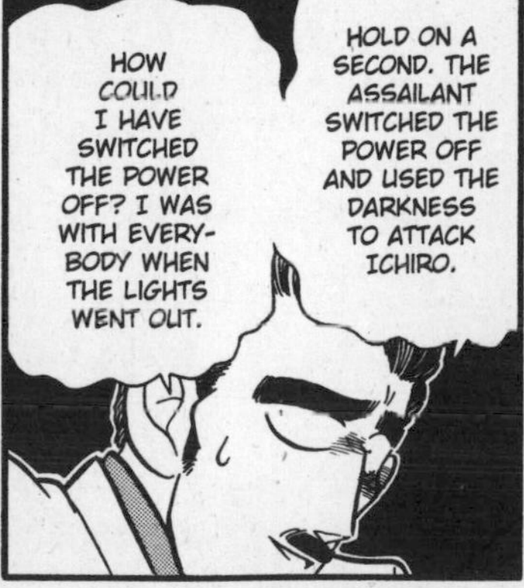
HOLD ON A SECOND. THE ASSAILANT SWITCHED THE POWER OFF AND USED THE DARKNESS TO ATTACK ICHIRO.
HOW COULD I HAVE SWITCHED THE POWER OFF? I WAS WITH EVERY-BODY WHEN THE LIGHTS WENT OUT.

THAT'S RIGHT.
THERE'S ONLY ONE PERSON WHO COULD'VE DONE THAT...

ACTUALLY, THAT'S NOT NECESSARILY SO.

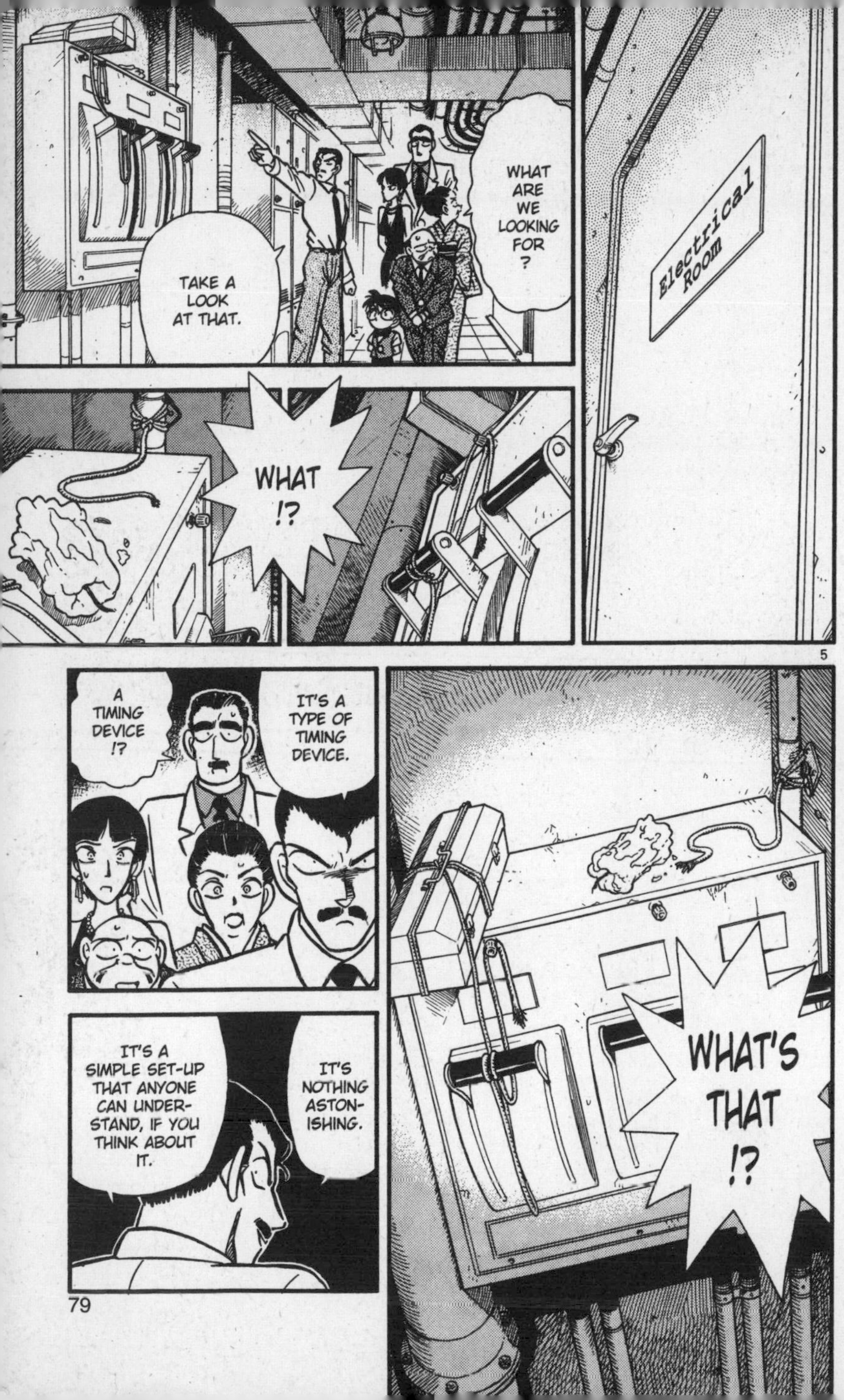

Electrical Room

WHAT ARE WE LOOKING FOR ?

TAKE A LOOK AT THAT.

WHAT !?

5

ATTACH A WEIGHT TO THE BREAKER AND KEEP IT FROM MOVING BY SECURING IT TO A FIXED POINT WITH A STRING THAT'S LOOPED AROUND A CANDLE PLACED IN BETWEEN.
AFTER SOME TIME THE CANDLE BURNS THE STRING, CAUSING IT TO SNAP.
SNAP
THE RELEASED WEIGHT BRINGS THE BREAKER DOWN AUTO-MATICALLY.
CRANK

THE EQUIPMENT USED TO MAKE THIS DEVICE WERE PROBABLY FOUND IN THE STORAGE ROOM.

JUDGING FROM THE SPENT CANDLE, I INFER THAT IT WAS SET UP SOME TIME AGO.
IN OTHER WORDS, ANYBODY COULD HAVE SWITCHED THE POWER OFF.

IT WOULD'VE BEEN POSSIBLE TO SET UP THE BLACK-OUT AND STAB ICHIRO AND STILL BE WITH US IN THE DINING ROOM WHEN THE LIGHTS WENT OUT.

ANY ONE OF YOU COULD HAVE DONE IT !!

OF COURSE, OUR MISSING FRIEND TAKESHI COULD HAVE DONE IT, TOO.

TIK
TIK
TIK

UNGH ...

DOES IT HURT, ICHIRO ?

TIK
TIK
TIK

ICHIRO ...

DASH
WHAM
DA DA DA

HUF
HUF
HUF
HUF
DARN... IF WE CAN'T FIND HIM AFTER ALL THIS SEARCHING ...
... MAYBE HE'S NOT ON THE SHIP ANYMORE.

BUT WE HAVEN'T LOOKED EVERY-WHERE YET.
HUH ?

YOU KNOW, EVERY ONE'S ROOMS.

TH- THAT'S UNLIKELY ...
HMM ... NOT ENTIRELY UNLIKELY.

LET'S GO TAKE A LOOK !
TH-THEN, SHALL WE START WITH MRS. MARIKO AND MR. KITARO'S ROOM?
TMP TMP TMP

CLACK
HMM, TAKESHI'S NOT HERE ...

HMPH ...

THIS COUPLE... THEY SEEM TO HAVE CONFLICTING PERSONALITIES. DO THEY GET ALONG WELL?
YES ...

THEY'RE COUSINS, YOU SEE.

THEY'VE GOTTEN ALONG WELL SINCE THEY WERE CHILDREN, THOUGH IT MIGHT NOT SEEM LIKE IT.

M-MARRIAGE BETWEEN COUSINS !?
YES ...
COME TO THINK OF IT, MR. GOZO FURIOUSLY OPPOSED IT THEN, TOO ...

OPPOSED IT THEN, TOO ...!?

BAWOOGAH

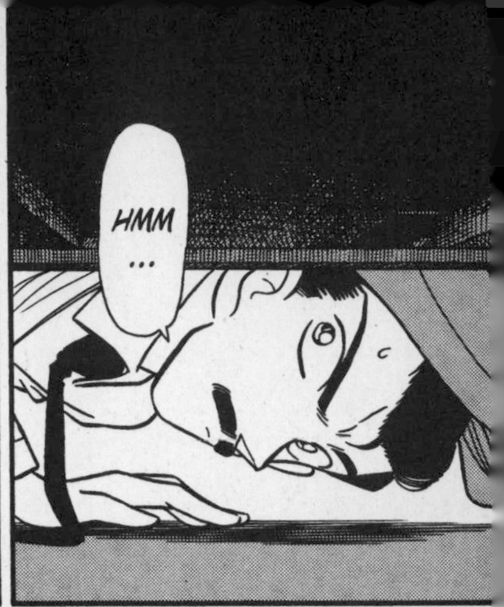
HMM
...

LOOKS LIKE HE'S NOT IN JOJI'S ROOM EITHER.
!?

HEY, DO YOU THINK THIS MIGHT BE HIS KNIFE CASE?
WHAT !?

TUNK
!?

THERE ARE TWO MISSING !!

WH-WHAT COULD THAT MEAN ?
WE FOUND ONE OF THEM WHEN ICHIRO WAS STABBED.
WHERE'S THE OTHER ONE?

.....

HEY! DON'T RUN IN SO CARE-LESSLY!!
LOOK, THERE'S A DRAWING!
TMP TMP ...

CLACK
HEY, THIS MUST BE ICHIRO'S ROOM!
Y-YES, BUT HOW--

TAKESHI COULD BE HIDING IN HERE WITH A WEAPON.

YEAH, RIGHT ...
MAYBE HE SKETCHED THE SCENE OF THE CRIME!
HA HA HA ...

FLIP
BUT HE REALLY IS TALENTED! ♡

HEY, KIDS. DON'T MESS AROUND IN OTHER PEOPLE'S STUFF!!
OKAY!

MM?

.....

WHAT ABOUT THIS?
OH, THAT'S ...

HEY, WHAT'S THIS?
IT'S CHAR-COAL!
IT'S USED FOR SKETCH-ING.

IT'S BASICALLY AN ERASER.
REALLY? COOL.
HEY! STOP DAWDLING OR I'LL LEAVE YOU BEHIND!!

HE'S NOT HERE, EITHER.
SEEMS THAT WAY.

HMM
...
BAWOOGAH

HE WASN'T IN OUR ROOM OR NATSUE'S ROOM.
FWP
AKIE'S ROOM HERE IS THE ONLY ONE LEFT.

BUT HE'S NOT HERE EITHER.

MAYBE HE ISN'T ON BOARD ANYMORE, AFTER ALL
...
CLICK

!?

SLAM
MM?

YOU FIND SOME-THING?
N-NOTHING AT ALL ...
HEH HEH ...

OH WELL. GUESS WE SHOULD GO BACK TO THE DINING HALL.
.....

HEY, MR. BUTLER?
YES?
BY ANY CHANCE, DID ...

PSSST PSSST
!?
... OR DID SOME-THING LIKE THAT EVER HAPPEN?

WHERE DID YOU HEAR ABOUT THAT? THE PERSON IN QUESTION, MR. GOZO, AND I WERE THE ONLY ONES WHO KNEW.
SO THAT'S IT.

I SUSPECTED AS MUCH !!

IN THAT FIRST INCIDENT WHERE MR. GOZO WAS KILLED IN HIS CABIN ...
WHY WERE THERE BREAD CRUMBS DROPPED AT THE CRIME SCENE?
AND WHAT HAPPENED TO THE WEAPON ?

THEN IN THE SECOND INCIDENT WHERE TATSUO WAS KILLED ON THE DECK ...
WHAT WAS THE MEANING OF THE SPLASH AND THE DULL THUD HEARD AT THE TIME THE CRIME WAS COMMITTED ?
AND WHO UN-LOCKED THE DOOR TO THE STORAGE ROOM ?

AND THEN THERE WAS THE THIRD INCIDENT, WHERE ICHIRO WAS STABBED IN THE DARKNESS !

NOW FINALLY, ALL THESE MYSTERIES ARE CONNECTED ...
... TO FORM A SINGLE THREAD !!

I MUST TELL EVERYBODY RIGHT AWAY.
ONCE THIS BOAT ARRIVES IN TOKYO, IT'LL BE OUT OF MY HANDS.

IT CAN'T BE HELPED. I'LL USE THIS THING DOC GAVE ME ...
UM, HEY ...
HUH ?
OVER HERE, OVER HERE ...

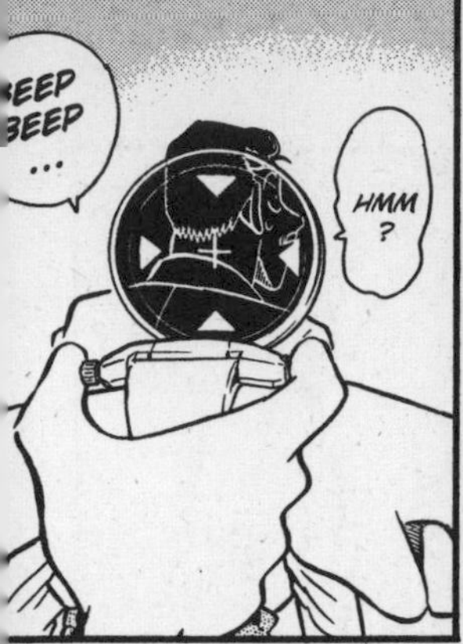
BEEP BEEP ...
HMM ?

POING

WHAT? DID YOU FIND SOME-THING ?

ZHOOP

PRICK

THUD
FWUMP ...
THIS IS CALLED A WRIST WATCH TRAN-QUILIZER GUN.

SORRY, OLD MAN ...
ZZZZ ...
AT CLOSE RANGES, YOU CAN USE IT TO PUT PEOPLE TO SLEEP INSTANTLY.

CLACK
HEY, WHERE'S DAD ?

HE SAID TO GATHER EVERYONE IN AKIE'S ROOM IN TEN MINUTES. HE HAS SOMETHING IMPORTANT TO SAY!
SOME-THING IMPOR-TANT TO SAY ?

THANKS, GUYS !!
DASH
UH, SURE ...

HURRY !
HURRY !!
HURRY !!!
AH-- AH--
THE OLD MAN'S VOICE WAS SETTING NUMBER 59, I THINK ...

CLACK

WHAT'S GOING ON, MR. DETECTIVE?
WHY DID YOU GATHER US ALL HERE?

I FINALLY FIGURED IT OUT.

WHAT ...?

A SERIES OF CRIMES HAS BEEN COMMITTED ON THIS SHIP.
AND I KNOW WHO THE CULPRIT IS ...

FILE 6: UNATTAINABLE DREAM

WHAT !?
YOU KNOW WHO THE MURDERER IS !?

YES ...
I KNOW WHO COMMITTED THE THREE CRIMES ON THIS SHIP.
WHO IS IT !?

TELL US! WHO'S THE MUR-DERER !?
IT HAS TO BE *HIM* !
IT'S ALL TAKESHI'S DOING, RIGHT !?

DON'T BE SO HASTY.
BEFORE I DISCLOSE THE NAME OF THE MURDERER, LET'S RE-EXAMINE THE THREE CRIMES.

IN THE FIRST INCIDENT, MR. GOZO WAS FOUND BLOODILY STABBED TO DEATH IN HIS CABIN WITH THE DOOR LOCKED FROM INSIDE.

FROM THE BLOOD FOUND IN THE GROOVE OF THE DOOR ...
...WE CAN DEDUCE THAT MR. GOZO WAS STABBED OUTSIDE HIS ROOM. HE THEN FLED BACK INTO HIS ROOM, LOCKED THE DOOR TO AVOID FURTHER ATTACK, AND PASSED AWAY.

A FLOWER WAS FOUND OUTSIDE THE CABIN.
YEAH! TAKESHI HAD THAT FLOWER ON, SO TAKESHI MUST BE THE MURDERER!

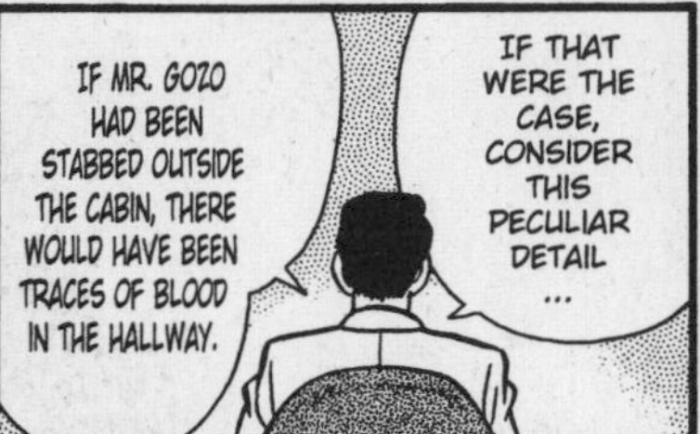
IF THAT WERE THE CASE, CONSIDER THIS PECULIAR DETAIL ...
IF MR. GOZO HAD BEEN STABBED OUTSIDE THE CABIN, THERE WOULD HAVE BEEN TRACES OF BLOOD IN THE HALLWAY.

COULDN'T THE MURDERER HAVE WIPED IT CLEAN TO DELAY THE DISCOVERY OF THE BODY?
Y-YEAH! IT DOESN'T CHANGE THE FACT THAT TAKESHI IS THE PRIME SUSPECT!
WHAT I'M TRYING TO POINT OUT IS NOT THAT THERE WASN'T ANY BLOOD OUTSIDE ...

... BUT THAT THE FLOWER WAS PLACED IN THE HALLWAY AFTER THE BLOOD HAD BEEN WIPED AWAY!!
!?

IT WOULD MAKE SENSE IF TAKESHI LOST THE FLOWER AS HE STABBED THE VICTIM, THEN HURRIED OFF TO FLEE THE SCENE.
BUT THE MURDERER CAREFULLY WIPED THE HALLWAY AFTER-WARDS.

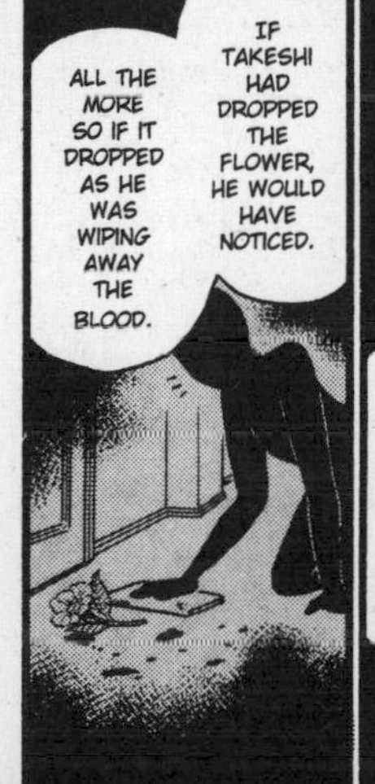
IF TAKESHI HAD DROPPED THE FLOWER, HE WOULD HAVE NOTICED.
ALL THE MORE SO IF IT DROPPED AS HE WAS WIPING AWAY THE BLOOD.

IN OTHER WORDS, THE MURDERER PLACED THE FLOWER THERE AFTER WIPING THE HALLWAY CLEAR OF BLOOD!
... TO MAKE IT LOOK LIKE TAKESHI DID IT!!

!?

NOW CONSIDER THE SECOND INCIDENT WHERE TATSUO WAS BEATEN TO DEATH ON THE DECK.
IN THIS INCIDENT, NEITHER THE MURDER WEAPON NOR ANY REAL EVIDENCE WAS LEFT BEHIND.
UNLIKE THE FLOWER IN THE FIRST CASE AND THE RIGGED BREAKERS IN THE THIRD, THERE WAS NO EVIDENCE OF PREMEDITATION.

IN OTHER WORDS, IF IT WAS INDEED COMMITTED BY THE SAME PERSON ...
I AM INCLINED TO BELIEVE THE SECOND CRIME WAS UNPLANNED.

THEN WHY WAS TATSUO KILLED ...?

THE KEY IS INSIDE THIS CASE.
FWIP
THAT'S ... THAT'S MY KNIFE CASE !!

FWAP
TAKE A LOOK. THERE ARE TWO MISSING!
ONE WAS FOUND AT THE SCENE OF THE THIRD CRIME... BUT WHERE'S THE OTHER?

A CRUCIAL POINT HERE IS THE SOUND CONAN REPORTED HEARING AROUND THE TIME OF THE SECOND MURDER.
HE HEARD A SPLASH FOLLOWED BY A DULL THUD.

THE THUD WAS PROBABLY THE SOUND OF TATSUO BEING HIT.
WHAT CAUSED THE SPLASH BEFORE THAT?

WHEN THE DULL THUD HAPPENED, THE MURDERER MUST STILL HAVE BEEN ON DECK, SO IT WASN'T THE SOUND OF THE MURDERER JUMPING INTO SEA.
SPLASH
THAT SUGGESTS IT WAS THE SOUND OF SOMETHING THROWN INTO THE SEA... AND IT'S REASONABLE TO THINK THAT MAY BE THE REASON TATSUO WAS KILLED.
NOW THEN... WHAT WAS IT THAT WAS THROWN INTO THE SEA?

IT COULD HAVE BEEN THE OTHER KNIFE MISSING FROM THIS CASE.
AND PERHAPS TATSUO HAD JUST HAPPENED TO SEE THAT...

IN SUM, TATSUO UNWITTINGLY WITNESSED THE DISPOSAL OF THE WEAPON USED IN THE FIRST MURDER.
TATSUO WAS MURDERED TO KEEP HIM SILENT. WITH THIS THEORY ALL THE PIECES FALL INTO PLACE!!

HAVE YOU FOR-GOTTEN? THE STORAGE ROOM WAS LOCKED FROM THE OUTSIDE.

IT WOULD HAVE BEEN IMPOSSIBLE FOR TAKESHI TO ESCAPE UNLESS SOMEBODY UNLOCKED THE DOOR FROM THE OUTSIDE.

I SEE ...
BUT AFTER THE SECOND MURDER, TAKESHI ESCAPED FROM THE STORAGE ROOM AND DISAPPEARED !!
YEAH! I STILL THINK TAKESHI IS SUS-PICIOUS !

THEN WHO --?
WHO OPENED IT !?

MOST LIKELY, THE MUR-DERER.
WHAT !?

ASSUMING MY THEORY IS CORRECT, THE SECOND MURDER WAS NOT PLANNED.
THE MURDER OCCURRED WHILE TAKESHI WAS STILL LOCKED UP IN THE STORAGE ROOM.
TAKESHI WOULD BE PROVEN INNOCENT AFTER ALL THAT WORK TO SET HIM UP AS THE PRIME SUSPECT.

THAT'S WHY THE MURDERER UNLOCKED THE DOOR.
TO CREATE A SITUATION WHERE IT WOULD BE POSSIBLE TO CONTINUE SUSPECTING TAKESHI OF THE CRIMES !!

WHY DON'T WE HAVE HIM EXPLAIN IT HIMSELF.
H-HIMSELF ...?
YOU FOUND TAKESHI !?

B-BUT IF TAKESHI'S NOT GUILTY, WHY DID HE RUN AWAY!?
Y-YEAH! AND HE'S STILL MISSING !!

TAKESHI... WHY DON'T YOU QUIT HIDING AND COME OUT?
H-HE'S HERE, IN THIS ROOM?

TAKESHI !!

CREAK
!?
CRRRREAK
TAKESHI ?

TAKESHI
!

NOW, TAKESHI, TELL US HOW YOU GOT OUT OF THE STORAGE ROOM.
......

START, SAY, WHEN NATSUE SAW TATSUO'S DEAD BODY ON THE DECK AND SCREAMED.
WHAT HAPPENED AFTER THAT SECOND INCIDENT !?

I ...
I THOUGHT SOMETHING HAPPENED TO NATSUE.

I HEARD NATSUE'S SCREAM COMING FROM THE DECK...
KYAAA
I WAS BESIDE MYSELF, AND WHEN I FRANTICALLY TRIED TO GET OUT ...
CLICK
... SOMEHOW THE DOOR WAS UNLOCKED, AND I WAS ABLE TO ESCAPE.

BY THE TIME I GOT TO THE DECK, EVERYBODY WAS GATHERED AROUND TATSUO'S DEAD BODY.

IT'S TAKESHI! TAKESHI DID IT AGAIN!!

...

I THOUGHT THEY WOULD TRY TO BLAME IT ON ME AGAIN SO I RAN AWAY, LOOKING FOR A PLACE TO HIDE ON THE SHIP.

THE DOOR TO AKIE'S ROOM HAPPENED TO BE OPEN SO I RAN IN...

I'VE BEEN HIDING IN THIS CLOSET THIS WHOLE TIME.

TAKESHI ...

HMM ...

THAT WOULD MEAN IN THE THIRD INCIDENT, ICHIRO WAS STABBED BY SOMEBODY ELSE.

THEN WHO DID IT !?
WHO'D DO SUCH A HORRIBLE THING TO MY ICHIRO !?

IT'S BECAUSE THE MURDERER'S PLAN DIDN'T WORK OUT.
PLAN ...?

WHEN THE MURDERER UNLOCKED THE DOOR TO THE STORAGE ROOM ...

... HE THOUGHT IT WAS A CLEVER WAY TO PUT THE BLAME ON TAKESHI.
BUT THE QUESTION OF WHO UNLOCKED THE DOOR FROM THE OUTSIDE LED TO TALK OF AN ACCOMPLICE.
INSTEAD OF BEING IN THE CLEAR, THE MURDERER WAS SUDDENLY ONE OF THE POSSIBLE SUSPECTS.

THE PANICKED MURDERER DEVISED A PLAN TO DIVERT SUSPICION AWAY FROM HIMSELF.
THAT WAS THE MOTIVE BEHIND THE THIRD CRIME, WHERE ICHIRO WAS STABBED IN THE DARKENED RESTROOM.

BUT IN COMMITTING THE THIRD CRIME, THE MURDERER DUG HIMSELF IN A HOLE !!

.....

ICHIRO, AFTER YOU WERE STABBED YOU SAID THAT ...
... IT WAS PITCH DARK AND YOU COULDN'T SEE THE FACE OR THE BUILD OF THE ASSAIL- ANT ...
YOU SAID THERE WAS NO LIGHT AT ALL.
Y- YES ...

IN ADDITION, TAKE THE FACT THAT THE WEAPON WAS FOUND AT THE SCENE.
UNLIKE THE FIRST AND SECOND CRIMES, THIS TIME THE SUSPECT DIDN'T ESCAPE WITH THE WEAPON.

THAT MEANS THE ASSAILANT COULDN'T SEE YOU, THE VICTIM, EITHER.
ISN'T IT DIFFICULT TO STAB SOMEONE WITHOUT ANY LIGHT? HOW DO YOU STAB A PERSON YOU CAN'T EVEN SEE?
BUT THE ASSAILANT ***KNEW*** YOUR PRECISE LOCATION AND MANAGED TO STAB YOU.

THAT IS TO SAY, THE SUSPECT WAS ***NOT ABLE*** TO FLEE WITH IT ...
... BECAUSE HIS LEG WAS WOUNDED AND HE COULDN'T MOVE.

WHAT !?
ARE YOU SAYING THAT --?
YES. THE PERSON WHO STABBED ICHIRO ...

GASP!
... WAS ICHIRO HIMSELF !!

AND THE PERSON WHO MURDERED MR. GOZO AND TATSUO WAS ALSO...
... ICHIRO !

YES! *YOU* DID IT !!

!?

I-ICHIRO ...?

.....

THAT'S ALL CONJECTURE!!
YOU DON'T HAVE A SHRED OF EVIDENCE THAT ICHIRO IS THE MURDERER!
HERE'S THE EVIDENCE.
FWIP
IT WAS FOUND AT THE SCENE OF THE FIRST MURDER, NEAR MR. GOZO'S BODY.
IT'S A BREADCRUMB.
B-BREADCRUMB!?

SOMEBODY MUST BE TRYING TO PIN THE MURDERS ON ICHIRO.
NO, THAT'S UNLIKELY.

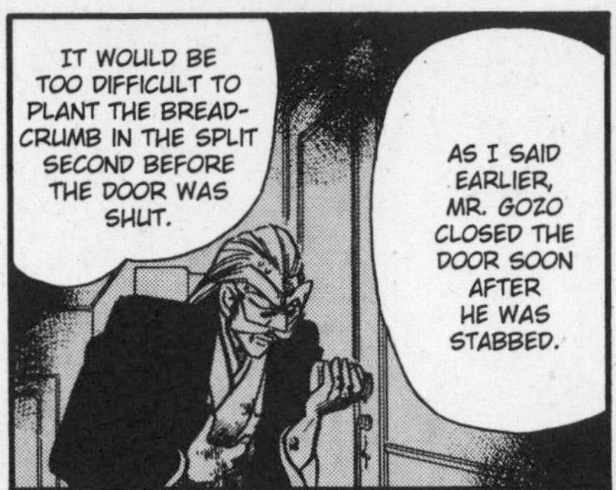
AS I SAID EARLIER, MR. GOZO CLOSED THE DOOR SOON AFTER HE WAS STABBED.
IT WOULD BE TOO DIFFICULT TO PLANT THE BREAD-CRUMB IN THE SPLIT SECOND BEFORE THE DOOR WAS SHUT.

IN OTHER WORDS, THE MURDERER DID NOT INTENTIONALLY PLACE THE BREADCRUMB THERE.
RATHER, THE MURDERER ACCIDENTALLY DROPPED IT!!

BUT HE HAS NO MOTIVE!!
ICHIRO HAD NO REASON TO KILL FATHER.
AH... THAT STUMPED ME AS WELL, UNTIL THE VERY END...
BUT THEN I FOUND SOME-THING IN ICHIRO'S ROOM.
WH-WHAT DID YOU FIND?
THIS...
ICHIRO KILLED MR. GOZO...
!?

AND HERE'S HIS MOTIVE!!!
TUNK

.....
A DRAWING?

H-HOW CAN A DRAWING BE THE MOTIVE...?
THE KEY IS THE SUBJECT OF THE DRAWING.

YOU SAY SUBJECT, BUT...
FLIP
S-STOP...

!?

HEY, THESE DRAWINGS...
THEY'RE ALL OF NATSUE!

HUH?

STOP IT!!
UNGH ...
I- ICHIRO ...
ICHIRO, YOU DIDN'T ...
YES ...
YOU SEE, ICHIRO ...
... IS IN LOVE WITH NATSUE.

I HEARD FROM SUZUKI, THE BUTLER...
YOU WERE UNABLE TO TELL NATSUE HOW YOU FELT FOR HER, SO YOU WENT TO MR. GOZO AND--
Y-YES, THAT'S RIGHT...

I ASKED HIM TO LET ME MARRY NATSUE!!
WHAT!?

...

I-ICHIRO...

BUT GRANDFATHER WOULDN'T ALLOW IT!!
HE WENT ON ABOUT HOW I WASN'T GOOD ENOUGH FOR HIS DEAR NATSUE...

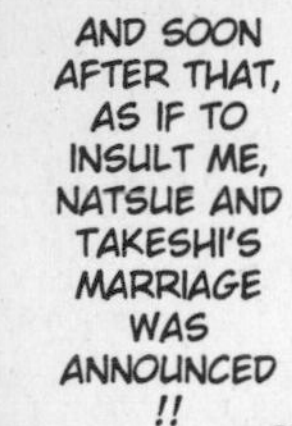
AND SOON AFTER THAT, AS IF TO INSULT ME, NATSUE AND TAKESHI'S MARRIAGE WAS ANNOUNCED!!

NOT GRANDFATHER, WHO REFUSED TO APPROVE MY MARRIAGE TO NATSUE...
AND NOT TAKESHI, WHO STOLE NATSUE AWAY.
I COULDN'T FORGIVE THEM.

AND...AND... THE WORDS GRANDFATHER SPIT OUT AT ME YESTERDAY WHILE I WAS SKETCHING NATSUE ON THE DECK.
IT'S TIME TO ABANDON UNATTAINABLE DREAMS!!

I COULDN'T FORGIVE THEM!!

ICHIRO'S CRY OF ANGUISH ECHOED THROUGHOUT THE SHIP.

SO IT WAS MISERY-- THE MISERY OF AN INTROVERTED YOUNG MAN UNABLE TO GIVE VOICE TO HIS DEEPEST FEELINGS-- THAT LED TO TRAGEDY.

THE SHIP SAILED CLOSER TO TOKYO.
IT GLOWED RED AS THE SUN SET ON THE SADNESS AND DESPAIR OF ICHIRO AND THE HATAMOTO FAMILY.

FILE 7: A STRANGE GIFT

HEY! IT'S A LETTER FROM NATSUE!

UM ...
DEAR MR. MOORE, RACHEL, AND CONAN. HOW ARE YOU ALL DOING?

I APPRECIATE WHAT ALL OF YOU DID THAT DAY.
I APOLOGIZE FOR RUINING WHAT SHOULD HAVE BEEN A HAPPY TRIP FOR YOU.

THREE WEEKS HAVE PASSED SINCE GRAND-FATHER AND TATSUO'S FUNERAL...
...AND EVERYBODY IS BEGINNING TO GET OVER THE SHOCK.

AFTER A LOT OF THINKING, TAKESHI AND I DECLINED GRANDFATHER'S ESTATE AND DECIDED TO CUT OUR TIES TO THE HATAMOTO FAMILY.
WE HAVE NOW BEGUN A NEW LIFE ON A RANCH IN HOKKAIDO.

I'VE ENCLOSED A PICTURE OF US.

WOW! ♡

IF YOU EVER COME TO HOKKAIDO, PLEASE STOP BY.

.....

I WONDER WHAT JIMMY IS DOING?
HE HASN'T CALLED IN A WHILE.
GASP

H-H-HE'S PROBABLY HAVING A HARD TIME WITH A CASE HE'S HANDLING.
BUT IT'S BEEN SUCH A LONG TIME... AND HE HASN'T BEEN AT SCHOOL EITHER.
HE WOULD'VE SOLVED ANY CASE BY NOW.

UNLESS ... C-COULD HE HAVE ...
HUH ...?

... LOST HIS TOUCH ?
.....

DING DONG

DING DONG
COMING!

CLICK
WHOA
FWOM

FWUNK
KYAA!
OH ...
ARGH !

PAR-DON ME.
I CAME HERE TO DISCUSS A CERTAIN MATTER.

I'M SORRY, YOUNG LAD.

!?

ARE YOU OKAY ?
UH-HUH ...

.....
SO, YOU HAVE SOME-THING TO DISCUSS?
Y-YES ... WELL ...

M-MONEY OUT OF NOWHERE !?

YES ...
SINCE ABOUT TWO YEARS AGO, SOMEONE'S BEEN SENDING ME TOYS AND MONEY EVERY MONTH.

THE SENDER USES A MADE-UP NAME AND ADDRESS. IT'S A BIT CREEPY.
HMM, TOYS AND MONEY, HUH...?

DO YOU HAVE ANY CHILDREN ?
YES... A SON WHO JUST TURNED FIVE...

THEN MAYBE A FRIEND IS ANONY-MOUSLY--
NO... I'VE ASKED FRIENDS, ACQUAINTANCES, RELATIVES...
BUT IT WASN'T ANY OF THEM.

JUST HOW MUCH MONEY HAVE YOU BEEN RECEIVING?
A MILLION YEN EVERY MONTH.
INCLUDING THIS MONTH, THE TOTAL COMES TO ¥25 MILLION.

¥25 MILLION !?

WHY DON'T YOU JUST KEEP IT?
I CAN'T ACCEPT IT... NOT WHEN I DON'T EVEN KNOW WHO IT'S FROM.

MY SON IS HAPPY TO RECEIVE TOYS EVERY MONTH, BUT...
...THE MONEY SCARES ME. I HAVEN'T TOUCHED ANY OF IT.

WELL THEN, YOU COULD JUST LEAVE THE MONEY WITH ME, AND I'LL--
DAD !!

ARE YOU SURE YOU DON'T HAVE ANY IDEA WHO'S SENDING IT?
Y-YES ...
.....

MAYBE IT'S A FORMER PATIENT OF YOURS, DOCTOR.

HUH ?
PATIENT ?

YOU'RE A SURGEON, AREN'T YOU?
ER ... YES.
THEN IT'S NOT SO STRANGE FOR YOU TO RECEIVE GIFTS FROM A PATIENT YOU HELPED!

T-TRUE... THAT WOULD EXPLAIN THINGS.

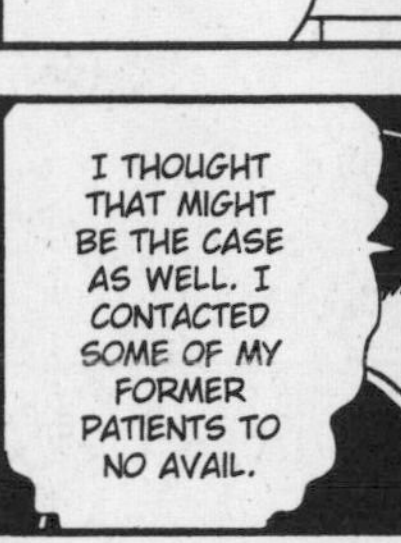
I THOUGHT THAT MIGHT BE THE CASE AS WELL. I CONTACTED SOME OF MY FORMER PATIENTS TO NO AVAIL.

.....

WAIT, DID I TELL YOU THAT ?
DID I MENTION I'M A SURGEON ?

!?

H-HOW DID YOU KNOW, CONAN ?
HIS INDEX FINGERS ON BOTH HANDS!
MY FINGERS ?

SURGEONS USE BOTH INDEX FINGERS TO TIGHTLY HOLD AND TIE SUTURES DURING SURGERY.
THAT LEAVES A MARK ON THE TIPS OF THEIR INDEX FINGERS.

YOU KNOW, THOSE DIAGONAL MARKS ON YOUR FINGERTIPS!

IT JUST SO HAPPENS THAT I PERFORMED AN EMERGENCY OPERATION THIS MORNING.

PLUS, YOUR HANDS STILL SMELL FAINTLY OF DISINFECTANT.
I-IS HE RIGHT?
Y-YES...

THAT WAS JUST LIKE...

YOU'RE QUITE AN OBSER-VANT BOY.
HEH HEH.
THIS LITTLE GUY KNOWS A LOT OF USELESS STUFF.
THAT'S AMAZING, CONAN!!

YOU'RE A GYMNAST AREN'T YOU?
H-HOW'D YOU KNOW ...?
GASP
THAT UNIQUE BRUISING ON HER THIGHS COULD ONLY BE FROM THE UNEVEN BARS...
OKAY, I ACTUALLY KNEW WHEN THE WIND BLEW HER SKIRT UP!
IT'S FUNDA-MENTAL FOR DETECTIVES TO BE OBSERVANT AT ALL TIMES...
LISTEN TO YOURSELF. YOU'RE A FRAUD! YOU KNEW **BEFORE** YOU EVEN SHOOK HER HAND!!
JUST LIKE ...

JUST LIKE JIMMY.

NOT A CHANCE.
BOING

NO, IT CAN'T BE.
BUT ...
TUG

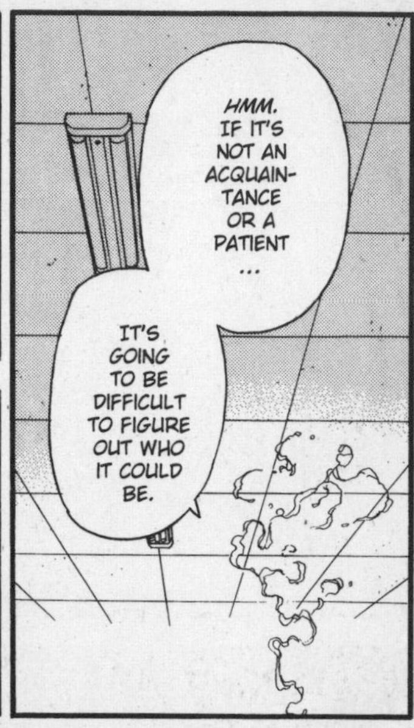
HMM. IF IT'S NOT AN ACQUAINTANCE OR A PATIENT ...
IT'S GOING TO BE DIFFICULT TO FIGURE OUT WHO IT COULD BE.

DO YOU HAVE ANYTHING ELSE FOR US TO GO BY?
WELL, I DON'T KNOW IF THIS WILL HELP OR NOT ...

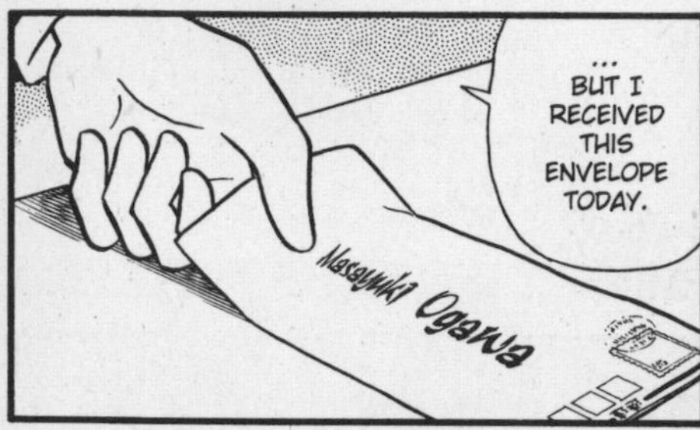
... BUT I RECEIVED THIS ENVELOPE TODAY.

HMM. NOTHING UNUSUAL ABOUT IT BESIDES THE MONEY INSIDE.
ACTUALLY THE MONEY USUALLY COMES WITH THE TOYS WRAPPED IN A BIG SHEET OF PAPER LIKE THIS.

TODAY FOR THE FIRST TIME, IT CAME IN THIS SMALL ENVELOPE ACCOMPANIED BY AN ODD LETTER.
LETTER ?

!?

I have now paid off the ¥25 million. I will come to complete the transaction.

YOU MEAN THE BAR-CODES!?

THAT IS STRANGE. ALL PRODUCTS THESE DAYS HAVE THEM, BUT MOST OF THESE HERE HAVE NO BARCODES.
YOU DON'T SEE TOYS LIKE THESE IN STORES THESE DAYS EITHER.

AND SOME OF THE TOYS ARE IN PRETTY BAD CONDITION.
.....

THAT'S RIGHT... SOME OF THE TOYS WERE SCRATCHED OR EVEN BROKEN WHEN I RECEIVED THEM.
WHAT!?

DOES THAT MEAN THE SENDER DOESN'T HAVE MUCH MONEY AND HAS BEEN STRUGGLING JUST TO BUY THESE USED TOYS FOR MY SON?
BUT THE SENDER IS RICH ENOUGH TO SEND A MILLION YEN EVERY MONTH!!
HE CAN CERTAINLY AFFORD TO BUY NEW TOYS!!

THIS MEANS HE'S DOING IT ON PURPOSE.

THE SELLER IS INTENTIONALLY SENDING YOU ITEMS THAT ARE EITHER USED OR WERE BOUGHT A LONG TIME AGO!!

NOT TO MENTION THE HUGE SUMS OF MONEY HE'S SENDING YOU!!

BUT ...

COULD IT BE POSSIBLE ...!?

COULD THIS BOY BE ...?

FILE 8: THE SAME PERSON

THERE'S NOTHING TO WORRY ABOUT, MR. OGAWA.
IT'S JUST A PRAC-TICAL JOKE.

Taro Tanaka
BUT THIS ADDRESS DOESN'T ACTUALLY EXIST, AND I DON'T RECOGNIZE THE NAME EITHER.
HMM... IF THE ADDRESS IS FAKE THEN THE NAME PROBABLY IS TOO.

THEN ALL WE HAVE TO GO BY IS ...
THE LETTER YOU GOT TODAY ENCLOSED WITH THE MONEY.

THIS LETTER'S OUR ONLY CLUE.
I have now paid off the ¥25 million. I will come to complete the transaction.
.....

HEY, COULD THE SENDER BE TRYING TO BUY SOMETHING FROM MR. OGAWA?
HUH ?

DEPENDING ON HOW YOU READ IT, THE LETTER COULD BE INTERPRETED THAT WAY.
Y- YOU'RE RIGHT.
.....

MR. OGAWA, DO YOU OWN ANYTHING WORTH APPROXIMATELY ¥25 MILLION ?
I DON'T HAVE ANYTHING CLOSE TO BEING THAT VALUABLE.
!?

COME TO THINK OF IT... THERE'S A PAINTING I INHERITED FROM MY GRAND-FATHER HANGING AT THE HOSPITAL WHERE I WORK.
I BELIEVE THAT THE PAINTING IS WORTH AROUND ¥20 MILLION.

BINGO !!!

THE SENDER MUST WANT TO BUY THAT PAINTING FROM YOU !!
WHAT !?
AND HE'S BEEN SENDING YOUR SON MONTHLY PRESENTS TO BUTTER YOU UP!!
THAT MUST BE IT !!!

LET'S GO TO THE HOSPITAL AND TAKE A LOOK AT THE PAINTING! MAYBE IT'LL GIVE US A CLUE!
WOULD THAT BE ALL RIGHT?
S-SURE, I DON'T MIND.

.....

BEIKA GENERAL HOSPITAL...
Beika General Hospital

WHAT A BIG HOSPITAL.
YES, I TOO WAS TAKEN ABACK WHEN I CAME HERE THREE YEARS AGO.
I TRANS-FERRED HERE FROM A SMALL COUNTRY HOSPITAL, YOU SEE.
THESE FLOWERS ARRIVED FOR YOU.
FROM A MR. TANAKA.

OH, DOCTOR OGAWA.
MM?
AGAIN THIS YEAR...
DID SHE SAY *MR. TANAKA*?

YES, IT'S THE SAME SENDER.
FOR THE PAST TWO YEARS I'VE ALSO BEEN RECEIVING THIS FLOWERING PLANT, BUT UNLIKE THE MONEY OR TOYS THIS GETS SENT TO THE HOSPITAL JUST ONCE A YEAR.
IT'S ALWAYS A MORNING GLORY ON AUGUST 3RD.

MORNING GLORY ?

IF THE SENDER IS GIVING YOU FLOWERS, MAYBE IT'S A WOMAN.
IF I REMEMBER CORRECTLY, IN THE LANGUAGE OF FLOWERS MORNING GLORY REFERS TO LOVE IN VAIN.

YOU WEREN'T... INVOLVED WITH SOME WOMAN TWO YEARS AGO, WERE YOU?
N-NO! DON'T BE RIDICULOUS !

THEN IS AUGUST 3RD SOME SORT OF SIGNIFICANT DAY? LIKE YOUR SON'S BIRTHDAY?
NO, MY SON YUTA'S BIRTHDAY IS IN DECEMBER. I CAN'T THINK OF ANYTHING ELSE EITHER.
.....

A MORNING GLORY SENT TO THE HOSPITAL ANNUALLY ON AUGUST 3RD...

HEY, MR. MOORE! HOW ABOUT TAKING A LOOK AT THE MEDICAL RECORDS OF HIS PAST PATIENTS?
HUH ?

MAYBE AUGUST 3RD HAS SOME-THING TO DO WITH A PATIENT.
UH, MAYBE SO ...
.....

MAY I TAKE A LOOK ?
OH, I CAN'T SHOW MEDICAL RECORDS TO OUTSIDERS!

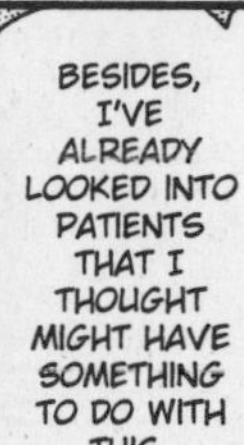
BESIDES, I'VE ALREADY LOOKED INTO PATIENTS THAT I THOUGHT MIGHT HAVE SOMETHING TO DO WITH THIS.

PLEASE !
.....

DON'T MENTION THIS TO ANYONE.
AH, THANK YOU.

File Room

FIND ANYTHING ?

MM ...
I BROUGHT OUT THE RECORDS ON EVERY SINGLE PATIENT I'VE HANDLED FOR THE LAST THREE YEARS.

YOU'RE SURE THAT NONE OF THESE PATIENTS WANTS THAT PAINTING ?
THAT'S RIGHT... I DON'T THINK IT COULD BE ANY OF THEM...

HMM ...
.....

WOULD YOU LIKE TO SEE THE ACTUAL PAINTING ?
I GUESS SO... MAYBE SOMETHING WILL COME OF SEEING IT.

IT'S HANGING IN THE WAITING ROOM.
I SEE.
.....
KCHK

C-CONAN, AREN'T YOU COMING?
NOPE! I'LL JUST WAIT HERE.

OH ...
OKAY ...

DON'T DISTURB ANY-THING.
I WON'T!

KCHK
THAT PAINTING IS VERY POPULAR WITH THE PATIENTS ...

KCHK

OH, MY ...

CONAN !?
FWIP
FWIP
FWIP
FWIP

FWIP FWIP FWIP FWIP
THAT'S SO ODD !!

HE'S ONLY IN ELE- MENTARY SCHOOL ...

THIS BEHAVIOR IS JUST TOO STRANGE !!

COME TO THINK OF IT, THERE WAS THAT TIME WHEN ...
WE'RE GOING TO HAVE TO INVESTIGATE EACH ONE ...
HEY, MR. MOORE, THOSE DOGS OVER THERE ...
AND THEN THERE WAS THE OTHER TIME ...
I THOUGHT IT WAS JUST A STATUE BUT IT'S ACTUALLY A LIGHTER! COOL!!
CONAN!
WHO'S THE KID?
AND THE OTHER TIME ...
ALWAYS ...
ALWAYS ...

THAT DAY ...
INSTEAD OF JIMMY BEING AT HIS HOUSE IT WAS...
... CONAN !?
IT COULDN'T BE POSSIBLE ...
COULD IT BE ...?
IS THIS BOY ...

IS HE ACTUALLY JIMMY !?
ONE WAY OR THE OTHER ...
I HAVE TO FIND OUT...
CLICK
I HAVE TO FIND OUT.
ALL RIGHT.

PHEW
...

HEY, YOU SHOULDN'T BE GETTING INTO THOSE FILES.
R-RACHEL ...

DID YOU FIND SOME-THING ?
Y-YEAH ...

YOU KNOW HOW MR. OGAWA SAID THOSE FLOWERS ARE SENT TO THE HOSPITAL ONCE A YEAR...?
AND ALWAYS ON AUGUST 3RD.
YES, GO ON ...
I THOUGHT MAYBE SOMETHING HAPPENED TO THE SENDER AT THIS HOSPITAL ON AUGUST 3RD.

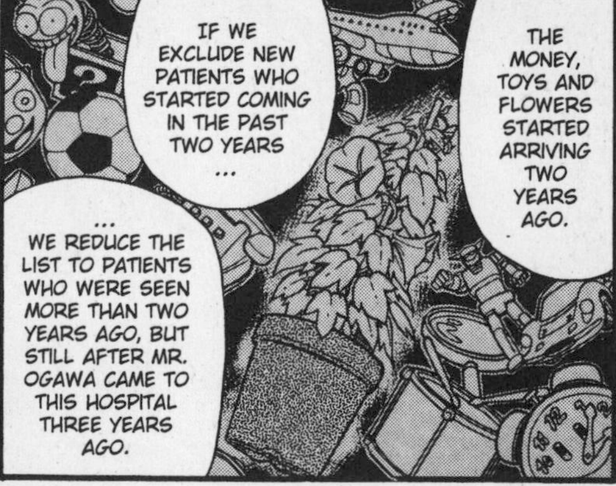
THE MONEY, TOYS AND FLOWERS STARTED ARRIVING TWO YEARS AGO.
IF WE EXCLUDE NEW PATIENTS WHO STARTED COMING IN THE PAST TWO YEARS ...
... WE REDUCE THE LIST TO PATIENTS WHO WERE SEEN MORE THAN TWO YEARS AGO, BUT STILL AFTER MR. OGAWA CAME TO THIS HOSPITAL THREE YEARS AGO.

OUT OF THOSE, THERE ARE EIGHT PEOPLE WHO HAD SOMETHING TO DO WITH AUGUST 3RD.
FOR EXAMPLE ...

THESE PEOPLE HAD SUCCESSFUL OPERATIONS THAT DAY ...

THESE WERE EITHER ADMITTED OR RELEASED THAT DAY ...

AND THIS PERSON ...

BUT IF YOU SEND FLOWERS AND GIFTS IT USUALLY MEANS YOU ARE GRATEFUL TO THAT PERSON, RIGHT?

I SUPPOSE SO.

CONSIDERING THE AMOUNT OF MONEY, THE SENDER IS EITHER ...

... MAKI OKADA, WHO HAD A SUCCESSFUL OPERATION ON AUGUST 3RD THREE YEARS AGO, OR ...

... HIROSHI WADA WHO LEFT THE HOSPITAL HAPPILY AFTER RECOVERING FROM A SERIOUS ILLNESS.

BUT SOMETHING STILL BUGS ME.

I have now paid off the ¥25 million. I will come to complete the transaction.

THAT LETTER ...

BUT IT'S IMPRESSIVE YOU FIGURED THIS MUCH OUT!!

NOT BAD ...

HUH !?

FILE 9: THE MYSTERY OF AUGUST 3RD

HUH
!?

AHA
!
I KNEW
IT! YOU
REALLY
ARE
...

...
JIMMY
!
WH-WH-
WHAT ARE
YOU
TALKING
ABOUT,
RACHEL
!?

M-M-MY
NAME'S
CONAN
!
CONAN
!!
OH,
NO
!!
.....

COME ON NOW... *HA HA HA...*

I'M FOUND OUT !!!

ALL RIGHT, IF IT'S COME TO THIS ...

THE TOYS MR. OGAWA BROUGHT !

WOWEE! A GAME-MAN! ♡
YAY! YAIBA'S BIG ADVEN-TURE!!
YAIBA
GAME MAN

THIS IS FUN! ♡
HA HA HA ! ♡
HE'S ...

GO YAIBA!! BEAT ONIMARU!!
.....
BLIP BLIP

BLIP BLIP
... PRE-TENDING !!!

NOW I'M EVEN MORE SUSPICIOUS! CONAN HAS GOT TO BE JIMMY.
BUT HOW'D HE GET SO SMALL?

THIS ISN'T SOME SCI-FI MOVIE.
SOME-THING THIS STRANGE ISN'T POSSIBLE.

!?

W-WAIT A SECOND...
CONAN, IS THERE SOMEONE SPECIAL YOU LIKE?
WHAT!?
BUT IF CONAN IS JIMMY...

I THINK I SAID...
WELL I HAVE SOME-ONE!!
YEAH?
AND HE SAID...
IS IT BY ANY CHANCE THAT JIMMY GUY YOU WERE LOOKING FOR?

YUP!
GASP!!
HE'S BEEN TEASING ME SINCE WE WERE KIDS AND ...
...SO SURE OF HIMSELF ...AND HE'S A DETECTIVE GEEK AND ALL...
OH ... NO!
BUT WHEN PUSH COMES TO SHOVE ...
HE'S BRAVE AND VERY COOL ...
AH ...
AH ...

I LIKE HIM SOOO MUCH! ♡

AAAAAAH!!!

MM
?
GAME MAN
Saved Games
1 Tomoya Ogino
2 Tomoya Ogino

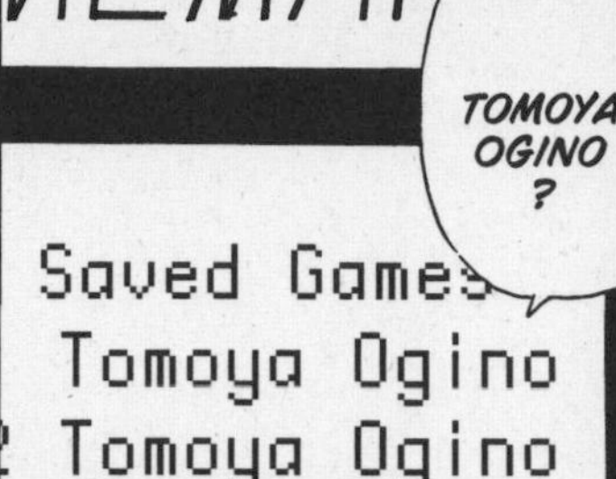
Saved Games
Tomoya Ogino
Tomoya Ogino
TOMOYA OGINO
?

I THOUGHT DOCTOR OGAWA'S SON'S NAME WAS...
... YUTA.

IF YUTA HAS BEEN PLAYING THIS GAME, HE'D ENTER HIS OWN NAME OR THE NAME OF ONE OF HIS FAVORITE CHARACTERS ...
WHO COULD THIS TOMOYA OGINO BE?
TOMOYA OGINO... I'VE SEEN THAT NAME SOME-WHERE ...

!?
THAT'S IT !!

I SAW IT IN THE MEDICAL FILES.
I'M SURE I DID ...
FLIP

YES, HERE IT IS! TOMOYA OGINO, AGE FIVE!!
DOCTOR OGAWA OPERATED ON HIM THREE YEARS AGO, BUT HE DIED... ON AUGUST 3RD!

WAIT A SECOND... DOCTOR OGAWA HIRED US BECAUSE OF...
...THE MONEY AND SECOND-HAND TOYS HE'S BEEN RECEIVING EVERY MONTH FOR THE PAST TWO YEARS.
AND THE SAME PERSON HAS ALSO BEEN SENDING FLOWERS TO THE HOSPITAL ON AUGUST 3RD EVERY YEAR.

AND TODAY, AUGUST 3RD, THE DOCTOR RECEIVED THAT LETTER WITH THE MONEY ...
I have now paid off the ¥25 million. I will come to complete the transaction.

!?
WHAT !?

COULD THAT LETTER MEAN ...?

RACHEL!! GET DOCTOR OGAWA IN HERE RIGHT AWAY!!

HUH?

NOW!!!

S-SURE...

DA DA DA

IT'S HIM!!

THE WAY HE TALKS, THE WAY HE ACTS, AND HIS POWERS OF DEDUCTION...

THERE'S NO MISTAKING IT.

THAT'S JIMMY!

I'M SURE OF IT!!!

WHAT! YOU KNOW WHO THE SENDER IS!?
File Room
HEY, ARE YOU SERIOUS?
IT MUST BE ONE OF THE PARENTS OF TOMOYA OGINO!!
THAT'S THE BOY WHO DIED THREE YEARS AGO FROM APPENDICITIS.
PEOPLE CAN DIE FROM APPENDICITIS?
IT'S RARE, BUT YES, IF IT'S NOT DISCOVERED IN TIME.
AND BY THE TIME THAT BOY WAS BROUGHT TO THE HOSPITAL, IT WAS ALREADY TOO LATE.
HIS FATHER HAD DIFFICULTY ACCEPTING THAT.

IT BELONGED TO TOMOYA OGINO, THE BOY WHO DIED THREE YEARS AGO!!
WHAT!?
IN OTHER WORDS, THE SENDER HAS BEEN SENDING DOCTOR OGAWA MEMENTOS OF HIS SON!!
THEY'RE GIFTS OF HATRED!!
AND THE FLOWERS THAT ARE SENT EVERY YEAR TO THE HOSPITAL ON AUGUST 3RD...
...ARE FLOWERS OF OFFERING FOR THE ANNIVERSARY OF HIS SON'S PASSING.
TH-THEN THAT LETTER...!
I have now paid off the ¥25 million. I will come to complete the transaction.
THE LETTER THAT ARRIVED TODAY...
YES...
MOST CER-TAINLY...

HE PLANS TO TAKE THE LIFE OF DOCTOR OGAWA'S SON!!

AND HE'LL DO IT TODAY, ON AUGUST 3RD, THE DAY TOMOYA DIED THREE YEARS AGO!!

WHAT !?
SOMEBODY ALREADY PICKED HIM UP!?

THEY TOLD ME HIS FATHER JUST PICKED HIM UP. ARE YOU SAYING IT WASN'T YOU, DEAR !?
TH- THIS CAN'T BE...

DARN !!
WE'VE GOT TO FIND HIS SON SOON, BEFORE...

HEY! WHERE'S THE KINDER-GARTEN ?
I-IT'S NOT TOO FAR FROM HERE.

THEN THEY MIGHT STILL BE CLOSE BY.
ALL RIGHT !!
H- HEY, CONAN !

BEIKA PARK...

HERE, BOY... A PRESENT FOR YOU!
WOW!

THANKS, MISTER!!

ARE YOU REALLY GONNA TAKE ME TO SOME-PLACE FUN?
OF COURSE...

I'LL TAKE YOU THERE REAL SOON...
GLINT

I'LL TAKE YOU TO ***WHERE TOMOYA IS*** ...

DA DA DA DA

FILE 10: THE NICK OF TIME

TOMOYA
...

YOU MUST'VE BEEN LONELY ALL THIS TIME.

BUT DON'T YOU WORRY, TOMOYA.
I'LL BRING A FRIEND TO YOU SOON, TOMOYA.

REAL SOON
...

DA DA DA DA DA DA

DA DA DA

WHERE ARE THEY!?

WHERE COULD THEY BE!?

IT HASN'T BEEN LONG SINCE HE ABDUCTED YUTA!!

THEY HAVE TO BE AROUND HERE SOME-WHERE!!

YUTA !!
TH-THERE !! IN THE PARK.
HUH ?
OH, NO !!
!?
ALL RIGHT, TIME TO USE 'EM ...
CLICK
CLICK
... THE SUPER SNEAKERS DOC GAVE ME ...
HUH !?
TMP

PONK
NO !!
BAM

FWOOOOSH
THWACK

?
CRASH
UNGH ...
KATUNK TUNK
WHAT THE --!?
!?
WHOMP
PHEW ...
DID ...
CONAN JUST DO THAT !?

YUTA !!
DADDY !!
TCH !
DASH

DON'T MOVE !!!
GRAB

NO ...
YOU KNOW WHAT'LL HAPPEN IF YOU MOVE.
!?
M-MR. OGINO ...

SO IT WAS YOU.
HMPH.

THAT'S RIGHT, IT WAS ME!! TOMOYA OGINO'S FATHER.
YOU BOTCHED HIS OPERATION AND KILLED MY SON THREE YEARS AGO!!!

IT WASN'T THE OPERATION!! WHEN HE WAS BROUGHT TO THE HOSPITAL IT WAS ALREADY TOO--
SHUT UP !!
YOU DON'T KNOW WHAT IT'S LIKE TO HAVE YOUR FIVE-YEAR-OLD SON KILLED.
YOU HAVE NO IDEA HOW IT FEELS TO BE A FATHER WHO LOST HIS ONLY SON.
MY PRECIOUS, PRECIOUS SON !!

I WAS LEFT WITH JUST MY SON'S ASHES ...
...AND THE ¥25 MILLION IN INSURANCE I HAD ON HIM.
THAT EXPLAINS THE ¥25 MILLION.
THAT'S RIGHT!! IN EXCHANGE FOR ¥25 MILLION, I WANTED THAT QUACK DOCTOR TO TASTE THE SORROW OF LOSING A SON!!
SO WITH BITTER HATRED I SENT YOU MY SON'S TOYS AND HIS FAVORITE FLOWER, THE MORNING GLORY !!

KILL *ME* INSTEAD !!
IF IT'LL MAKE YOU FEEL BETTER, KILL *ME* !!
PLEASE, NOT MY SON ...
NOT MY SON ...
OH! SO ***YOU'RE*** THE ONE WHO SENT ME ALL THOSE TOYS!!

THANK YOU, MISTER!! I PLAY WITH THEM ALL THE TIME!!

!?

TOMOYA ?

TOMOYA ...

RACHEL! CALL THE POLICE RIGHT AWAY !!
SOB
O-OKAY ...

I KNEW ALL ALONG THAT IT WASN'T BECAUSE OF A MISTAKE IN THE OPERATING ROOM.
I KNEW... SOB

WAIT !! DON'T CALL THE POLICE.
WHAT ?
BUT YOUR SON! HE TRIED TO...

I KNOW HOW HE FEELS ...
I CAN UNDER-STAND.

I MAY BE A DOCTOR, BUT FIRST AND FORE-MOST...

I, TOO, AM A FATHER.

THANK GOODNESS IT DIDN'T TURN INTO A HORRIBLE INCIDENT.
YEAH ...

BUT WHY DID HE TAKE TWO YEARS TO SEND ALL THE MONEY AND TOYS?
HE COULD'VE SENT IT ALL AT ONCE.

HE PROBABLY WAITED UNTIL DOCTOR OGAWA'S SON TURNED FIVE...
... THE AGE TOMOYA WAS WHEN HE DIED THREE YEARS AGO.
TONK
AH, I SEE.

GREAT DEDUCTION, AS USUAL.
GASP
HUH ?

HA HA HA ... BUT I'M JUST A KID SO ALL THIS IS PRETTY CONFUSING.
.....

I, UH, JUST REMEM-BERED SOME-THING I HAVE TO DO!
DASH
YOU GUYS GO AHEAD WITH-OUT ME !!

WHAT'S WITH HIM ?
.....

I'M HOME!!
RICHARD MOORE P.I.

HEY, WHERE'S YOUR DAD?
HE WENT OUT FOR A DRINK.

OH...

YOU MUST BE HUNGRY.
I'LL FIX YOU SOMETHING RIGHT AWAY!
OKAY!

OH YEAH...
I FORGOT TO TELL YOU...

I HEARD MR. KISHIDA, THE P.E. TEACHER, IS GETTING MARRIED.
REALLY...

THAT GORILLA, HUH?

CLICK

HUH?

HOW DO YOU KNOW ABOUT A TEACHER AT MY HIGH SCHOOL?
C-CUZ YOU ALWAYS TALK ABOUT HIM! YOU CALL HIM THE GORILLA ALL THE TIME ...
STOP LYING!!

I KNEW SOME-THING WAS FISHY.
YOU *ARE* JIMMY, AREN'T YOU!?
TH-THAT'S CRAZY ...

NOW FESS UP ...
... JIMMY !!!
UM ...
UH ...

BRRRRING

.....

BUT ...

JUST LEAVE IT ALONE !!

TH-THE PHONE ...

BRRRRRRING

BRRRING

HELLO, RICHARD MOORE PRIVATE INVESTIGATOR'S OFFICE...

FWP

DON'T TELL ME YOU'VE FORGOTTEN MY VOICE ALREADY !

GRIN

BUT JIMMY IS--

NO WAY ...

AH, YOU COLD-HEARTED LASS ...
JEEZ, THAT JIMMY ...
PLEASE, DOC!! RACHEL'S ON TO ME! USE THE VOICE MODULATOR AND CALL RACHEL.
THE THINGS HE MAKES ME DO!
ARE YOU LISTENING, RACHEL?
RACHEL ?
.....
HMPH
I'M SUCH AN IDIOT! I MUST'VE BEEN OUT OF MY MIND!
EVERY-THING'S FINE ...
TH-THANKS, DOC.
PHEW
BUT, JIMMY, WHY ARE YOU TALKING LIKE AN OLD MAN?
HA HA HA ...
UH-OH ...

☼BONUS PAGES☼

ALCOHOLIC DETECTIVE YUTAKA TANI SERIES FILE 257

TRAGEDY OF MISTER A

The Murder of Gosho Aoyama

Detectives:
Yutaka Tani
Masaki Negishi
Eiichi Yamagishi
Koichi Kishida
Keiji Aso

The Victim:
Gosho Aoyama

Puppet Play Detective Yamachan's We're All Friends

Not Chubby But Rather Fat Detective Masaki Negishi Mr. Aoyama Won't Wake Up

Murder Detective Keiji Aso

Aoyama Dies Twice

Find the Big Head Detective Kishi-Ko!

Hello, Aoyama here.

Because Conan plays soccer, I've become engrossed in Serie A of the World Cup. Also, I'm planning to form my own soccer team. I'm going to call the team "A.C. Conan." My favorite team is Juventus. Go Baggio!

A NOTE FROM THE EDITOR:
Conan's name obviously pays tribute to mystery authors Arthur Conan Doyle and Edogawa Rampo. Last volume we also learned that Richard Moore's name in the original Japanese version, Kogoro Mori, is a tribute to Edogawa Rampo's famous detective, Kogoro Akechi. Another naming reference that may not be so apparent is Conan's friend and confidant, Dr. Agasa. The doctor's name most likely pays tribute to mystery author Agatha Christie—the Japanese pronunciation of "Agatha" is indistinguishable from "Agasa." Although some of these references have been left out due to the name changes of some of the main characters, there are still many references left in the pages of this manga. Can you figure out what they are?

HERCULE POIROT

You all must have heard of queen of the mystery novel Agatha Christie and her creation, the famous detective Hercule Poirot and his "little gray cells"! During World War I, Poirot escaped from Belgium to England where he started working as a private investigator. Whenever anyone mistakes him for a Frenchman he always corrects them and informs them that he is Belgian. As he fiddles with his waxed mustache he often boasts of how he is the world's greatest detective. He cuts such a humorous figure you just can't dislike him. Poirot considers investigating the physical details of a crime scene to be child's play and is quite disdainful of doing such things. Instead, Poirot sits down in a chair and carefully listens to his client's story and uses his "little gray cells" to see through the mystery of a case. The clarity of his deductions never ceases to amaze my little pink brain cells!! I recommend reading ***Death on the Nile.***

LOVE MANGA?

LET US KNOW WHAT YOU THINK!

OUR MANGA SURVEY IS NOW AVAILABLE ONLINE. PLEASE VISIT: VIZ.COM/MANGASURVEY

HELP US MAKE THE MANGA YOU LOVE BETTER!